£2.80

THE
SCOTTISH
FARMERS'
MARKET
COOKBOOK

THE SCOTTISH FARMERS' MARKET COOKBOOK

NICK PAUL

First published by the Angels' Share
an imprint of
Neil Wilson Publishing
303 The Pentagon Centre
36 Washington Street
Glasgow G3 8AZ

Tel: 0141 221 1117
Fax: 0141 221 5363
E-mail: info@nwp.co.uk
www.nwp.co.uk
www.angelshare.co.uk

A catalogue copy for this book is available from the British Library.

ISBN 1-903238-72-2

Typeset in Sabon
Designed by Belstane
Printed in Finland by WS Bookwell

CONTENTS

6. Cakes and Slices

FOREWORD

Where does your food come from? Who's grown it, harvested it, processed it and is now selling it? You see it on the supermarket shelf looking in its prime, neatly labelled and carefully packaged. But who's actually produced it? Is it a local farmer with a small crop of, say, a traditional apple variety which only lasts for about four weeks in autumn? Probably not. Chances are, the apples have been trucked (or flown) halfway round the world at below zero temperatures – possibly picked unripe – from sources which can reliably keep the shelves filled throughout the year.

In the second half of the 20th century this highly sophisticated retailing system may have revolutionised the food we eat, but it has also divorced the food buyer from the farmer and producer. The scandal of BSE in the late 90s further compounded this gulf. So today, if you care about where your food comes from – who's grown it, harvested it and is now selling it – the better place to look is not on the supermarket shelf but at your local farmers' market.

For it's here that you can sense again the natural seasons; have a friendly face to answer your questions, knowledgeably, about where and how the food has been produced; and also feel the joy of freshness which is an inspiration to get into the kitchen and start cooking.

For centuries – before the modern retailing revolution – market produce led and inspired cooks. And for farmers and their wives 'market day' was a vital part of their weekly routine. Taking whatever produce was ripe and ready for sale to market, it was their 'day out'; a time to socialise with friends or have a bit of fun once everything had been sold. Perhaps even take a wee refreshment, which truth found honest Tam o' Shanter – 'as he frae Ayr ae market night did canter.'

The revival of the old farmers' markets have brought back life and fun to town and city streets. They have made a vital reconnection with the land and its produce. All that remains is that buyers are inspired to cook, which is why I welcome this timely book.

Catherine Brown, 2004

INTRODUCTION

The Farmers' Market Philosophy – fresh Scottish produce, sold in season and sold by local producers! It's as simple as that.

It is so easy today to create meals by shopping at Farmers' Markets, which provide all the best in vegetables, meat, game, poultry, fish, eggs, fruit, jams and more. You can find ingredients that have all the true flavour and goodness of fresh produce rather than the brightly-coloured, chilled and re-packaged goods found in the supermarkets, that promise so much but often fail to deliver.

Scotland has an enviable reputation for producing some of the finest foods in the world: nearly all the langoustines eaten in Spain are from the West Coast of Scotland; Scottish Aberdeen Angus has long been the byword for quality meat; Scottish raspberries and tayberries are arguably the finest available and so the list goes on! Local growers and producers are supplying Markets from the Borders up to Orkney, as indeed they have for hundreds of years.

There is now a movement away from the global produce offered by the supermarkets and a return to the seasonality of food. People are once again realising that, for example, fresh Brussels sprouts – crunchy, sweet and straight from the stem – are a wonderful vegetable accompaniment. Quickly cooked for a few minutes in a wok with a little sesame oil, they are worlds away from the grey, flavourless overcooked 'school dinner' horrors of the past!

Farmers' Markets in Scotland combine a greengrocer, butcher, garden centre, off-licence, game dealer and delicatessen, craft shop and more, bringing them all under one 'roof'. The produce available includes homemade meat pies; wild, fresh line-caught fish; oat cakes and biscuits with the flour milled by water wheels; honey, herbs and cheese. You have the opportunity to speak to the farmer or producer about their passion for bringing the finest stock to the Market and they will happily offer suggestions and tips for getting the best out of the goods. If you are unsure about the meaning of the term 'organic' or if you only know one way to cook sausages, at the Market, there is always helpful advice on hand from the producers themselves.

Today, agriculture is moving away from the intensive practices of recent years. Although there is still a place for mass-produced products, many farmers are looking towards quality produce and small scale production methods, and are utilising natural fertilisers and pesticides wherever practical. For example, farms are growing potatoes with chicken manure as fertiliser. Similarly, weeds are being kept under control by turning the soil instead of automatically spraying, or using biological methods of pest control. This re-emergence of free-range practices focuses on and ensures the health and well-being of livestock. Animals are being given more space to avoid overcrowding and so, by the simplest of means, the spread of disease is reduced. Rare breeds are also being reintroduced, as people recognise the great taste and high quality that they provide, which has been all but lost from the mass-produced herds.

Intensive chemical farming, once promoted as the saviour of cheap food, is becoming a thing of the past as we turn more and more towards the quality of the food, realising that the cost is no longer prohibitive. The benefit to the environment is also apparent, as fewer chemicals are allowed into the water table and pollutants are reduced – this benefits both wildlife and the public as a whole.

It is also difficult to balance the demand for organic produce with, for example, the argument of the 'green mile'. That is, it is fine to have an organic bean along with its perceived better taste but, if the beans have to be imported from as far away as South Africa or South America, the cost in terms of distribution surely outweighs the benefits of the produce. Buying locally grown and produced items firstly reduces the need for transportation, so the process is less harmful to the environment in terms of the amount of distribution required. There are benefits for the actual livestock as well, as this decrease in the transportation process lessens the stress on the animals. In addition, localised production processes ensure the safety of local employment.

Shoppers insisting on 'organic' produce quite often fail to understand that there are still chemicals and pesticides used in the production of these goods. However, these are usually specific chemicals which have been approved for use by the Soil Association. The labelling may say one thing but, speaking to the farmers, you may be surprised to find that many of the methods employed are in fact equivalent to organic methods. It often turns out that the farm has elected not to go wholly organic in practice for reasons such as stocking processes or packing.

Imported fruit and vegetables are very often the choice of supermarkets because they need varieties that have thick skins for handling, or are able to be harvested un-ripe for transportation in gas-filled containers that artificially ripen the stock enroute to the warehouses. The quality of food depends on more factors than simply if a pesticide or chemical has been used in its production. You should always look for mature, ripe and fresh produce.

The same applies with meat or fish. If the producer can tell you the age of the lamb or venison, or if the fish is freshly caught, where it came from and when landed, this ensures the consistency and guarantee of quality. Farmers at

Farmers' Markets are interested in more than simple shelf-life of goods. They will bring to Market sufficient produce to sell that day, often producing or harvesting their stock just a day or so before. This means that no extended storage times and no unnecessary preservatives are used in the production process. Again, this reinforces the farmers' intention that, with the minimum of fuss, the produce is fresh and ready for the table.

With the use of simple methods such as poly-tunnels, which in their most basic form are just plastic sheets stretched over a rigid frame, growing seasons can be extended. This allows growers to crop some produce earlier than nature intended but, having been grown in the soil and warmed by the sun, the end result is still a natural, tasty item. It is also offered on a seasonal basis which is the best way to enjoy food; in season and at its very freshest.

Delicious strawberries, fresh hand-dived scallops and superb trout; real, thick cream, beef, lamb or poultry direct from the farm; herbs and vegetables that are literally still sprouting on the stall, fine beers and liqueurs – the range of choice covers just about all you need to create superb simple meals with all the goodness of quality, fresh ingredients. And all from one shopping trip! Don't forget the trimmings on offer as well: wonderful fresh flowers and pure beeswax candles for the table, chutneys, chocolates and treats to impress!

The purpose of this cookbook is to demonstrate that fine cooking need not be complicated, and that shopping at the Farmers' Market for your ingredients will provide the best flavours and guarantee a fresh, quality meal. A few of the recipes call for the inclusion of specific spices or a limited number of goods that may not be on sale at all of the Markets. Generally though, you may well find that these 'extra' ingredients are ready to hand.

There are tips and suggestions for a variety of recipes here. If you would like to contact any of the growers or producers, there is a directory at the rear of the recipe section with their contact details and a list of the markets attended. We hope you find this useful. Some of the producers will only attend with certain items on a seasonal basis, so be prepared to see those goods only at specific times of the year. If you have enjoyed any of the goods from a particular supplier, please tell them at the Market!

Don't forget to take this book with you when you go shopping, and enjoy the recipes.

Nick Paul, 2004

Carrot and Chervil Soup

Chervil can be eaten raw in salads and goes really well with chicken dishes as a nice alternative to parsley, coriander or tarragon. It can also be combined with other herbs to enhance their flavour.

Cook's Tip: Chervil is full of vitamin C, but to retain its goodness, only add towards the end of cooking.

275g/10oz carrots, chopped
50g/2oz butter
50g/2oz plain flour
1L/2pt chicken stock
½ cup chervil, chopped
Salt and pepper to season
Fresh cream to garnish

MAKING: Melt the butter in a pan and cook the carrots for five minutes. Stir in the flour, add the stock and season to taste. Boil, reduce the heat and simmer for 30 minutes. Remove from the heat, allow to cool slightly, pour into a blender and puree. Return to the pan with the chopped chervil and slowly return to the boil.

FINISHING AND SERVING: Stir, remove from the heat and serve, hot or cold. Garnish with a splash of fresh cream or, if serving cold, stir in some yoghurt in place of the cream, as it is a lighter finish. Top off with a couple of sprigs of fresh chervil.

Cullen Skink

BY NELLIE PIRIE

Cook's Tip: Try adding a little turmeric to the stock to increase the colour if preferred.

Smoked haddock, skinned and boned
900g/2lb potatoes
1 medium onion
1L/2pt milk
300ml/½ pt fresh cream
300ml/½ pt water
25g/1oz butter
1tsp parsley
Salt and pepper to season

MAKING: Thinly slice the potatoes and the onion and place in a pan with 300ml/½ pt of water. Place the smoked haddock on top of the vegetables and steam gently until the fish and vegetables are cooked, for about 10-12 minutes. Add the milk, cream, parsley and butter, season to taste and simmer slowly for ten minutes.

FINISHING AND SERVING: Remove the pan from the heat and transfer its contents to a serving dish. Serve with warm crusty bread, snip some chives over the top for a garnish, or sprinkle over some paprika.

Game Soup

Cook's Tip: You can make this soup in advance and reheat when required, or freeze for use later. If freezing, use within three months.

Yield: 4-6 servings

1L/2pt beef stock
1 pheasant, partridge or pigeon carcass
1 forequarters of rabbit or hare
1 medium carrot, quartered
1 medium onion, quartered
4 bay leaves
1 lemon, juiced
50ml/2fl oz port
Salt and pepper to season

MAKING: Place the stock, game carcass, forequarters, carrot, onion and bay leaves in a large pan. Bring to the boil, cover and simmer for about one hour until the meat is tender. Strain the liquid, reserving the carrot, onion and pieces of meat, in order to remove fat from the stock as well as any small bones. *Note: The meat will fall off the bones while simmering and can be lifted out of the pan with a slotted spoon. Add the meat to the reserved vegetables and discard the bones.* Place the carrot, onion, pieces of meat and the stock liquid in a blender and puree to the desired consistency.

FINISHING AND SERVING: Return the mixture to a clean pan, season to taste, add the lemon juice and port and reheat. Serve hot with crusty bread. For added taste try stirring in a little redcurrant jelly and a splash of thick cream. Croutons can also be added.

Leek and Potato Soup

4 leeks, washed, trimmed
30g butter
3 floury potatoes, chopped
750ml/1¼ pt chicken or vegetable stock
250ml/½ pt milk
Pinch paprika
Salt and pepper
Fresh cream to garnish
Fresh Parsley

MAKING: Wash the leeks thoroughly and cut into small pieces. Heat the butter in a pan and fry the leeks for about three to four minutes until softened. Add the potato and stock, boil and continue cooking at a simmer for about 20 minutes. Cool and pour into a blender and puree the mix. Do this in batches if required.

FINISHING AND SERVING: Return to the pan, add the milk and paprika and reheat. Adjust the seasoning if required and serve hot. This needs little more than some fresh bread for accompaniment. Add a garnish of fresh parsley or a swirl of cream for visual effect.

Oatmeal Soup

FROM HEATHERSLAW CORN MILL

This is a really warming and very simple soup.

Cook's Tips: Try adding a little carrot or potato for even more texture! If you have any leftover lamb or chicken, dice the meat and add to the soup. To vary the flavour a little, add a small amount of crushed garlic, or sprinkle some fresh herbs, such as chopped fennel leaves, meadowsweet or chervil, over the top before serving.

1 large onion
1 large carrot
1 leek
1 small turnip
1tbsp oil
25g/1oz medium oatmeal
600ml/1pt stock (chicken or vegetable)
450ml/³/₄ pt milk
Salt and pepper to season
Chopped parsley

MAKING: Chop the vegetables into small, evenly-sized pieces and put in a pan with the oil. Cook the vegetables until the onion is transparent and stir in the oatmeal. Fry gently for five minutes. Add the stock and simmer for 45 minutes, stirring occasionally.

FINISHING AND SERVING: Add the parsley and season to taste. Just before serving, add the milk and gently reheat. Serve with a good crusty loaf for a filling meal.

Onion, Carrot and Stilton Soup

FROM KNOWES FARM

350g/12oz onions, chopped
1 large carrot, sliced
1 stick celery, chopped
300g/10oz potatoes, peeled and diced
100g/4oz Stilton cheese, crumbled
50g/2oz unsalted butter
1L/2pt chicken stock
Salt and pepper

MAKING: Melt the butter in a large pan and gently cook the onion, celery and carrot until the onion is transparent. Add the diced potatoes, stir well and add the stock. Bring to the boil and simmer for 15 minutes. Season to taste, remove from the heat, pour into a blender and liquidise. Return to the heat and stir in the Stilton cheese.

FINISHING AND SERVING: Heat through and stir until the cheese melts. Serve at once with crispy croutons and a side salad with a blue cheese dressing.

Parsley Soup

FROM KNOWES FARM

Cook's Tip: Increase the amount of coriander a little if preferred.

250g/8oz flat leaf parsley, including leaves and fine stalks, rinsed and chopped
2 large carrots, chopped
1 large onion, chopped
1L/2pt chicken stock
40g/1³/₄oz unsalted butter
10g/1tsp coriander
Salt and pepper
Crème fraiche to garnish

MAKING: Melt the butter in a large pan and add the onion and carrots, cooking gently until the onion is transparent. Do not allow to colour. Add the parsley and coriander a third at a time and stir until the leaves have wilted. Place the chicken stock in a separate pan, season, bring to the boil and pour over the vegetables. Simmer for ten minutes. Remove from the heat, pour into a blender and liquidise.

FINISHING AND SERVING: Return to the heat, taste and adjust the seasoning. Serve hot and garnish with a swirl of crème fraiche alongside a good crusty bread. Add a garnish of curly leaf parsley if desired.

Arbroath Smokie Paté

FROM IAIN R SPINK, ARBROATH
PREPARED BY KEVIN GRAHAM

This is an easy starter to prepare ahead of time and reserve in the fridge – remove half an hour before serving.

Cook's Tip: Use low-fat cream cheese for a reduced calorie option.

1 pair smokies, boned and skinned
225g/8oz Philadelphia cream cheese
150ml/¼pt double cream
½ lemon, juiced
Pinch cayenne pepper
Salt & pepper to taste

MAKING: In a blender, liquidise the smokies, lemon juice and cayenne pepper and then transfer the mixture to a mixing bowl. Add the cream cheese and mix well with a wooden spoon until smooth. Add the cream and seasoning to taste.

FINISHING AND SERVING: Spoon into small ramekins, cover with foil and chill for two hours. Serve with hot toast fingers, oatmeal biscuits or with a lightly-toasted seeded loaf. For a tasty light meal try a fresh salad with lemon wedges and dress the salad with some fennel seeds to compliment the flavour of the paté. An additional option is a salad of finely-diced onion, radish, carrot, tomato and shredded lettuce leaves seasoned with coriander leaf and stalk with one diced red chilli pepper, finished with salt and pepper to taste and a squeeze of lemon juice.

Beetroot and Goats' Cheese with Orange Juice

FROM THE CRISP HUT
BY MAUREEN WALLACE

Cook's Tips: Add a little fresh basil leaf, some toasted brown breadcrumbs or toasted pine nuts to the cheese before cooking for added flavour and texture.

4 'rounds' of fresh goats' cheese
1 medium fresh, cooked beetroot   not preserved in vinegar – grated
25ml/2fl oz fresh orange juice
Salt and pepper to season

MAKING: Place a small amount of the beetroot, sufficient for each person, onto a heat-proof plate. Drizzle a little of the orange juice over the beetroot. Top with one round of goats' cheese per plate. Place under a hot grill until the cheese browns around the edges and slightly melts onto the beetroot.

FINISHING AND SERVING: Season and serve at once. Use a contrasting colour plate, such as dark blue, for a wonderful visual effect and top with fresh parsley and coriander leaves.

Blue Cheese in Breadcrumbs

Cook's Tips: Try a couple of different types of firm cheeses, such as Strathdon Blue, Bellevue Goats Blue or Brodick Blue, for a variety of textures, colours and flavours. Be sure not to use too soft a cheese, as it will melt while cooking.

100g/4oz blue cheese
1 egg white, beaten lightly
50g/2oz white flour
50g/2oz white breadcrumbs
10ml/2tsp oil

MAKING: Cut the blue cheese into four equally-sized pieces. Cubes would be best, however if you are using alternative shapes, be aware that they may cook unevenly depending on the thickness of the cheese, resulting in a very soft 'thin' end and a firmer 'thick' end. Dip the cheese (using cocktail sticks if preferred) into the beaten egg white, flour and then into the white breadcrumbs so that there is a good covering over the majority of the cookable surface. Brush a little oil on to a hot pan and place the cheese, breadcrumb side down, into the oil. Cook until the breadcrumbs have just browned, then carefully remove from the pan.

SERVING: Serve on a white plate, with the breadcrumbs facing up, alongside a crusty bread, or oatcakes, and a salad including roasted pine nuts for texture. Served over warm cherry tomatoes, heated in a moderate oven and sprinkled with olive oil and rosemary is a delicious variation too.

Cheese Soufflé

FROM STICHILL JERSEYS

Yield: 4 servings as a starter or 2 servings as a main course

150g/4½ oz Stichill Kelsae cheese
30g/1oz butter
30g/1oz plain flour
150ml/¼ pt milk
¼ tsp salt
¼ tsp pepper
5g/¼ oz English mustard powder
4 large eggs, separated
15g/½ oz Parmesan cheese (optional)

Preheat the oven to 190°C/375°F/Gas 5.

MAKING THE SOUFFLÉ: Melt the butter in a medium saucepan, stir in the flour and cook gently for one minute. Gradually add the milk and bring to the boil, stirring all the time until very thick and smooth. Remove the pan from the heat and crumble in the Kelsae cheese, salt, pepper and mustard powder. Mix well and leave to cool for a couple of minutes then, one at a time, beat in the egg yolks. Whisk the egg whites until stiff and glossy, but not 'dry'. Add 2-3tbsp of the whisked whites to the cheese sauce and stir until the sauce is thinned to about the same consistency as the whisked egg whites. Gently fold in the remaining egg whites and pour the mixture into a buttered 2½ pt soufflé dish. Sprinkle the top with the Parmesan (if using) and bake in the centre of the oven for about 30 minutes or until well risen, golden and just set.

MAKING THE BALSAMIC DRESSING: Combine 1tbsp chopped hard-boiled egg, 1tbsp chutney, ¼ tsp curry powder, 1tbsp fresh lemon juice, ½ cup olive oil, 3tbsp balsamic vinegar, a pinch of salt and pepper and 1-2tbsp of crumbled Kelsae cheese in a mixing bowl. Simply stir all together and refrigerate until required. Stir again before serving.

FINISHING AND SERVING: Remove the soufflé from the oven and serve immediately with a fresh green salad and a balsamic dressing (see above). A nice granary bread would go well with this, or even a flavoured loaf such as olive or tomato bread, warmed with a little extra cheese on the top.

Easy Devilled Eggs

FROM KINTALINE PLANT AND POULTRY CENTRE

Use separate mixing bowls if you wish to serve a variety of flavours, with the following as a few suggestions:

1. Finely-chopped smoked salmon and dill
2. Sweet chilli sauce and tomato puree
3. Crumbled-up cooked crispy bacon and parsley
4. Grated blue cheese and finely diced celery with a dash of Tabasco sauce
5. Spinach, coriander and curry powder
6. Cooked salmon, lemon juice, parsley and sour cream
7. Grated cheese, Worcestershire sauce and diced cooked smokey bacon
8. Finely sliced ham with slices of spring onion and a little of your favourite mustard

Cook's Tip: Use eggs that are at least four days old, as the eggshell can stick to the whites if the eggs are very young.

Quantity of eggs as required
1L/1³/₄ pt cold water
Fresh mayonnaise, crème fraiche or yoghurt
Salt and pepper to season

BOILING THE EGGS: Add a little salt to the water in a large pan and bring to a full boil. Place the eggs in the water and keep at a boil, allowing nine to ten minutes to achieve a firm, hard-boiled result. *Note: Do not place too many eggs in the water at one time, as this will lower the cooking temperature of the water too much.* Cook the eggs in small batches if cooking a large quantity for a meal.

PREPARING THE EGGS: Cool the eggs under cold, running water, and peel off the shell. On an open plate, slice the eggs in half lengthways and remove the yolk into a separate bowl.

MAKING THE EGGS: Add the mayonnaise, crème fraiche or yoghurt to the egg yolks, season with a little salt and pepper and mash together, but do not over mix. Add your choice of seasoning to the yolks and return a small portion to each halved egg white.

FINISHING AND SERVING: Decorate the finished eggs with some chopped chives, parsley or paprika. Use the finished eggs as a garnish on top of a salad as a main meal, or use as a treat for a picnic.

Extra Scrambled Eggs

Cook's Tips: Add a few fresh chives to the beaten eggs or some fresh basil leaves. The smoked duck can be varied by using smoked venison cut into very thin strips or, for a stronger flavour, other smoked meats, such as wild boar. This also works well with smoked fish – trout or salmon for example.

3 eggs, beaten
60g/2oz smoked duck
1 small onion, finely chopped, or 2 small shallots
½ small clove garlic, crushed
2 cherry tomatoes, chopped
Pinch chilli powder
Pinch coriander leaf
Knob unsalted butter
Salt and pepper to season

MAKING: Heat a pan and melt the butter. Add the onion or shallots, garlic, tomatoes, chilli and coriander and fry for a few minutes until the onion is transparent, but do not allow to colour. Add the beaten eggs and stir over a low heat until the eggs just start to set. Add the smoked duck and finish cooking the eggs to 'soft scrambled'.

FINISHING AND SERVING: Remove from the heat and serve at once, accompanied by brown bread or on toast made from wholemeal bread.

Porridge

There are two types of porridge that you can make, using either pinhead oats or flaked oats. Both are extremely easy to prepare.

Cook's Tips: To make a real winter warmer add a dram of whisky! To make the pan easier to clean, fill with cold water immediately after cooking. Do not leave the pan to dry out as the oatmeal can set solid!

PINHEAD OAT PORRIDGE

4tbsp pinhead oatmeal
600ml/1pt water
Pinch salt

MAKING: Sprinkle the oatmeal into the water in a large pan and mix well using a wooden spoon or traditional spurtle. Leave to soak overnight. Next morning, transfer to a double pan and cook for approximately 30 minutes, adding the salt to taste. To prevent sticking, gently stir occasionally. If the porridge is too thick, add a little boiling water.

SERVING: For a richer option, serve with fresh double cream and sprinkle a little soft brown or Demerara sugar over the top.

OATMEAL PORRIDGE

2-2½ cups of milk, a mixture of water and milk or just water, if preferred
1 cup of oat flakes
Pinch salt

MAKING: Place all the ingredients in a medium pan and bring to the boil, stirring constantly to prevent sticking. Cook for approximately one and a half minutes.

SERVING: Serve with a dash of cold milk. For a richer option, serve with fresh double cream and sprinkle a little soft brown or Demerara sugar over the top.

Scallops with Trout and Leeks

Cook's Tips: For a further flavour, add a little crushed garlic to the leeks and shallots. To colour the scallops, put a little sugar on top of each and place under a very hot grill for a few seconds. This will give the effect of searing, and the caramelised sugar will add a nice 'crunch' to the dish. If you do not have a griddle to put bar marks on the scallops, heat a metal skewer and quickly press it onto the top of them. Use the roe – the pink of the scallop – as well as the white meat for this recipe.

12 fresh scallops
1 small leek, washed and cut into thin strips
2 shallots, chopped
100g/4oz smoked trout, flaked into small pieces
10ml/2tsp oil
½ lemon, juiced
Salt and pepper to season

MAKING: Heat the oil in a small pan and add the leek and shallots, frying quickly until the shallots are transparent. Heat a griddle and trickle a few drops of oil onto the hot surface. Place the scallops on the griddle and cook for no more than one minute per side, to just seal them. Finally, add the smoked trout pieces to the leek and shallot mixture.

SERVING: Place three scallops onto each serving dish, place some of the leek, shallot and trout mixture next to them and add a few drops of lemon juice. Season and serve at once with fresh brown bread. If you have the shells for the scallops, to vary the presentation, pile some of the cooked leek, shallot and trout mixture into one shell per portion and top with the scallops.

Smoked Breast of Duck
with Wild Mushrooms

FROM TOMBUIE SMOKEHOUSE
BY SALLY CRYSTAL

Cook's Tips: Because the sauce is very rich, you may wish to use crème fraiche in place of the cream. A few fresh redcurrants or diced pieces of apple as a garnish will dress the lettuce leaves, as well as add to the presentation.

Yield: 8 servings

1 breast smoked duck (approx 225g/8oz) from Tombuie Smokehouse
30g/1½oz dried wild mushrooms
4 slices brown bread
200ml/¹/₃ pt fresh cream
1tbsp dry sherry
1tbsp olive oil
2tsp apple or redcurrant jelly
Handful of mixed lettuce leaves

MAKING: Slice the duck breast into thin strips and divide into eight portions. Soak the dried mushrooms in water for 25 minutes, drain and set aside. Slice the mushrooms, put them into a pan with the olive oil and add the sherry. Fry for two minutes. Add the apple or redcurrant jelly and simmer for five minutes. Cut the bread slices into quarters and fry in a different pan until crisp. Stand the bread on end in the pan and allow to drain and cool. Add the cream to the mushroom sauce and heat gently. Do not boil or overheat.

FINISHING AND SERVING: Remove the fried bread from the pan and top each slice with a portion of duck. Spoon the mushroom sauce around the duck and garnish with the mixed lettuce leaves. Serve at once.

Arbroath Smokie 'en Papillote'

FROM IAIN R SPINK, ARBROATH
PREPARED BY KEVIN GRAHAM

Cook's Tips: Use greaseproof paper in place of the foil and open the parcel at the table for the full effect of the aroma. Try with one of the lemon-thyme or pineapple-sage herbs for different flavours.

1 pair smokies
4 slices tomato
75g/3oz mushrooms, sliced
½ lemon, juiced
25g/1oz butter
Pinch parsley
Pinch thyme
Freshly-ground black pepper

Preheat the oven to 175°C/350°F/Gas 4.

MAKING: Gently warm the smokies, split and remove the bones. Place the fish on a piece of greased baking foil. Season with the pepper and squeeze over the lemon juice. Lay the four slices of tomato in a row lengthways, top with the sliced mushrooms and sprinkle with parsley and thyme. Melt the butter and pour over the top. Seal each smokie individually, making a parcel, and cook for ten minutes.

FINISHING AND SERVING: Remove from the oven, open each parcel and arrange on a presentation dish. Garnish with lemon slices and fresh parsley and serve at once. As an accompaniment, try serving with a fresh salad and oven-baked cherry tomatoes. Cook these on a baking sheet in the oven, with the stalk left on and just a touch of olive oil so that the skin of the tomatoes crinkles and the flesh is warmed through.

Baked Stuffed Onions

Cook's Tip: For a vegetarian option, omit the bacon and use a vegetable stock.

4 large onions, skinned
60g/2oz finely diced smokey bacon, rind off
45g/1½oz rolled oats
60g/2oz cheddar cheese, grated
15g/½oz blue cheese, grated
1tsp Worcester sauce
6tbsp beef stock
Salt and pepper to season

Preheat the oven to 160°C/325°F/Gas 3.

PREPARING THE ONIONS: Boil the onions in a large pan of water for 20-25 minutes. Remove from the water and slice off the tops with a sharp knife. Take out the centres but reserve the smallest (the rest of the centres can be used in stock or soups).

PREPARING THE STUFFING: Cook the diced bacon until very crispy. Mix the bacon with the blue cheese, oats, cheddar cheese, reserved chopped onion centre and Worcester sauce and season well. Divide the stuffing and place into each hollowed onion shell.

BAKING AND SERVING: Grease a shallow baking dish and pour in the stock (there should be sufficient liquid to cover the base of the dish). Put the stuffed onions into the baking dish, cover and place in the oven for 1-1½ hours or until tender. Serve this as a main course with extra green vegetables.

Beef in Brammle Sauce

FROM CAIRN O'MOHR WINERY
BY EDITH MOWATT

Cook's Tips: Try red cabbage cooked with a dash of white wine vinegar and raisins or diced apple as a side dish. Slice the cabbage thinly and steam with the vinegar and raisins or apples for a few minutes so that the cabbage is still crispy. No extra water is required as there is sufficient moisture in the vegetable. If the sauce appears a little 'dull', whisk in a knob of butter to give it a gloss before serving. Seasoning can be added if desired, but be careful not to add too much salt, as this will conflict with the flavour of the brambles in the Brammle Puree.

1 fillet highland beef
6 shallots, sliced in half
12 shiitake mushrooms, sliced
300ml/½ pt beef stock
300ml/½ pt Cairn O'Mohr Brammle Puree
10ml/2tsp oil
Handful of fresh brambles

FRYING THE BEEF: Cut the fillet into 2cm thick slices. Heat the oil in a pan and fry the fillet to preferred liking: two to three minutes per side for rare; two to four minutes per side for medium and four to five minutes per side for well-done. *Note: A good fillet should never really be cooked to 'well-done'!* Remove from the pan and transfer to a serving dish and keep warm.

MAKING THE SAUCE: Add the shallots and mushrooms to the pan used for the beef and fry for five minutes. Add the Cairn O'Mohr Brammle Puree and deglaze the pan by adding a little stock and heating the pan while scraping any 'bits' off the bottom. Slowly add the stock to the pan and boil to reduce the liquor by half.

SERVING: Pour the sauce over the beef and decorate with a handful of fresh brambles. Serve with sweet potato mash with chives and some crispy cabbage.

Beef Sausages with Wild Mushrooms Poached in Red Wine

Cook's Tips: For variety, use any type of meat sausages, such as venison, wild boar or lamb, or a combination of these. Add a few seasonal herbs to suit, such as thyme or oregano. Try adding a little redcurrant jelly before reducing the sauce. If the sauce looks a little 'dull', stir in a knob of butter to gloss before serving.

Beef sausages for 4 persons
1 medium onion (or 2 small shallots), sliced
150g/5oz mixed, fresh, wild mushrooms
1 clove garlic, crushed
200ml/7fl oz red wine
200ml/7fl oz beef stock
Salt and pepper to season
Oil for frying

MAKING: Skin the sausages and cut each into four pieces. Heat the oil in a pan and fry the onion and garlic gently until the onion is transparent. Chop the mixed wild mushrooms and add to the pan, frying for one minute. Add the sausage pieces and increase the heat, stirring all the time until the meat is browned. Add the wine and hot beef stock, season to taste and simmer until the meat is cooked through and the sauce has thickened. This should take about 20 minutes. Stir occasionally to avoid burning the bottom of the sauce.

FINISHING AND SERVING: Remove the sausage pieces from the pan and boil the sauce until thickened. Put the sausage pieces back into the sauce, and serve with mashed potatoes and seasonal vegetables. Serve over rice, a black and white mix, for example, or a red rice for a more 'nutty' finish.

Buchan Beef with Tomatoes, Onions and Elderberry Wine

FROM CAIRN O'MOHR WINERY
BY EDITH MOWATT

Cook's Tip: If using dried herbs, reduce the amount, as these have a stronger flavour than fresh ones.

450g/1lb best beef steak
1 medium onion, chopped
6 tomatoes, halved
1 red pepper, chopped
150ml/¼ pt elderberry wine
150ml/¼ pt beef stock
1tbsp olive oil
1tbsp clear honey
1tsp fresh basil
1tsp fresh oregano
1 level tsp cornflour diluted with water
Salt and pepper to season

MAKING: Cut the beef steak into equally-sized small pieces and brown evenly in the olive oil. Remove the meat from the pan and add the onion, tomatoes and red pepper, frying for five minutes or until just softened. Return the beef to the pan and add the elderberry wine and beef stock. Simmer for 15 minutes then add the herbs and stir. Simmer for a further 15 minutes and check the stock. If it is too thin, add the cornflour paste and stir well to thicken, cooking for a further five minutes. Once thickened, add the honey and stir.

SERVING: Serve at once with fresh bread or new potatoes finished in butter. Alternatively, try with new potatoes topped with a sour cream and chopped chive dressing. Sugar-glazed baby carrots and turnips would also go well with this recipe.

Chicken and Leek Pie

Cook's Tips: Add a few chives or tarragon to the pie mix to add to the flavour. Make individual pies by using small pie dishes. For this, reduce the cooking time to about 15-20 minutes.

1 cooked chicken, jointed (or use leftover chicken pieces)
2 medium leeks, washed and sliced
1 small onion or 2 small shallots, chopped
1 clove garlic, crushed
60g/2oz butter
30g/1oz plain flour
300ml/½pt chicken stock
125ml/4tbsp cream
1 sheet puff pastry
60ml/2tbsp milk
Salt and pepper to season

Preheat the oven to 200°C/400°F/Gas 6.

MAKING: Melt the butter in a pan and gently fry the onion (or shallots) with the leeks and garlic until the onions are transparent. Sprinkle in the flour, mix well and gradually add the stock, stirring to avoid lumps. Stir in the cream and add the cooked chicken, seasoning to suit. Pour into a pie dish and brush the edge of the dish with a little milk. Cut a circle out of the pastry to cover the dish, and lay it over the filling. Trim off any overhanging pastry and brush the top with the milk using a pastry brush. Make a couple of holes in the top of the pie to let out any steam. Bake for 25-30 minutes or until the pastry is golden and crispy.

SERVING: Serve at once with boiled potatoes and seasonal vegetables, with braised celery or chicory or with baked potatoes filled with sour cream and chives. As an alternative, serve with potato wedges. For this, parboil a couple of potatoes, cut into wedges and bake in the oven in a little oil. Add a spicy coating to them by rubbing on some chilli powder and salt, Cajun spice mix or cayenne and turmeric.

Chicken Breast Rolls with Bacon

This recipe will also work well with thin pork or veal escalopes, or turkey steaks, beaten out until thin.

Cook's Tips: Add a little crème fraiche to the sauce to make it creamier. For a different sauce, add a little Amaretto Liqueur and a few crushed almonds to the recipe or add some olives to the sauce (green or black) before reducing. Try substituting the basil with either a purple leaf basil or lemon-thyme. Use a couple of different coloured cheeses in one roll for effect and add spinach leaves to the parcels before rolling to increase the colour.

4 chicken breasts
100g/4oz cheddar cheese, sliced
4 rashers smokey bacon, rind off
8 fresh basil leaves
50g/2oz butter
300ml/½ pt chicken stock
Pinch paprika
Pinch fresh parsley
Salt and pepper to season

MAKING: Place the chicken breasts on a piece of clingfilm, cover with a second piece and gently beat out flat. Place one rasher of bacon and a couple slices of cheese on the chicken breast and add two basil leaves. Season with a little salt and pepper. Roll up the chicken breast over the bacon and cheese and seal with a cocktail stick to make a cylindrical parcel. Heat the butter in a pan and add the chicken parcels. Brown gently all over. Add the stock to the pan, together with the paprika and fresh parsley, bring to the boil and simmer for 20 minutes to poach the chicken.

FINISHING AND SERVING: Remove the chicken from the pan and keep warm. Boil the remaining liquid to thicken, scraping the base of the pan to lift the sediment, and adjust the seasoning. Place the chicken parcels on a serving dish, remove the cocktail stick and pour over the sauce. Serve at once with plain boiled rice.

Chicken Breast with Smoked Salmon and Goats' Cheese Filling

Cook's Tip: Try placing the filled chicken breasts on top of a fresh crisp salad with a lime and ginger dressing. For this, mix lime juice with a little shredded fresh ginger and soy sauce, and a little sugar and oil to finish.

4 chicken breasts, fillet removed
50g/2oz smoked salmon pieces, cut very small
50g/2oz goats' cheese
5g/¼ tsp freshly-ground black pepper
2 eggs, beaten
20g/1oz fresh breadcrumbs
20g/1oz flour
20ml/4tsp milk
10g/¼ oz tarragon
15g/¼ oz butter
15ml/1tbsp oil

PREPARING THE CHICKEN: Wash the chicken and dry off with a paper towel. Remove the small fillet from the rear of the breast (to use in other recipes). Cut a slit in the thickest part of the meat to make a small pocket.

PREPARING THE FILLING: Mix together the smoked salmon pieces, goats' cheese and tarragon to make a loose paste and season with a little pepper.

MAKING: Carefully stuff the pocket in the chicken breast with a little of the paste and tuck the edge of the meat over to seal. Beat the eggs into the milk. Dip the stuffed chicken breast into the flour, then the egg and milk mixture and then the breadcrumbs. Mix the butter and oil in a pan and heat gently. Place the coated chicken breasts in the pan and gently cook them in the butter and oil until the meat is browned all over and cooked through. This should take approximately 20 minutes.

SERVING: Serve with new potatoes and butter-glazed carrots. A fresh crusty bread with seeds would also be suitable to accompany this recipe.

Chicken Breasts Stuffed with Kelsae Cheese and Herbs in Puff Pastry

FROM STICHILL JERSEYS

Cook's Tips: Try using a purple leaf basil or lemon-thyme for a subtle extra flavour. Add some spinach leaves to the parcels before wrapping in the pastry.

4 chicken breasts
90g/3oz Kelsae cheese, sliced
Few sprigs of tarragon, sage leaves or other herbs of your choice
1 sheet puff pastry per chicken breast
Melted butter
Salt and pepper to season

Preheat the oven to 200°C/400°F/Gas 6.

MAKING: Place the chicken breasts on a board and carefully cut a pocket in the thickest part of the breast. Place a couple of slices of Kelsae cheese in the pocket and add a few herbs, seasoning with a little salt and pepper. Wrap the chicken breast in puff pastry and seal with a little melted butter, brushing over the top as well. Cut a slit in the top of the pastry to allow steam to escape and place on a baking sheet in the preheated oven for 20 minutes.

FINISHING AND SERVING: Remove from the oven once golden. To check that the chicken is cooked through, pierce the flesh with a sharp knife. The juices should run clear. If there is any sign of 'pink', continue cooking for a further few minutes and check again. Serve at once with steamed potatoes and vegetables of your choice. Roasted beetroot would go well with this or try a simple salad of shredded white cabbage and shredded carrot with a little oil dressing. For further flavour, use an oil infused with herbs such as thyme, basil or rosemary.

Chicken Forrestiere

FROM KINTALINE PLANT AND POULTRY CENTRE

Cook's Tip: For a different flavour, try adding some grated hard cheese or some prepared mustard or herbs, such as rosemary or thyme, to the mash.

1 whole chicken, divided into portions or individual pieces of wing, breast, etc
25g/1oz butter
2 bacon rashers per portion of chicken
2 medium mushrooms per portion of chicken
2 tbsp plain flour
150ml/¼ pt dry white wine
150ml/¼ pt double cream
Salt and pepper to season

Preheat the oven to 200°C/400°F/Gas 6.

MAKING: Cut the butter into small knobs and divide in half. Place one half all over the base of a flat, ovenproof dish (with sides of at least 2.5cm/1in) large enough to take the number of chicken portions to be cooked, and set to one side. Take two slices of the bacon and lay them side by side on a flat board. Slice one mushroom per portion and lay half of this over the bacon. Place the chicken portion over this and then top with the rest of the sliced mushroom. Fold the bacon slices up and over the chicken and mushroom to make a parcel, and place in the buttered dish with the join facing the base. Repeat this process for all the portions to be served. Place the remaining knobs of butter over the chicken then slice the second mushroom and place the slices over the butter and chicken. Season with salt and pepper and cover loosely with foil.

BAKING: Bake in the oven for 40 minutes. When ready – check that the juices of the chicken run clear by piercing the thickest with a skewer – strain the juices into a heavy-based pan and keep the chicken portions warm in a serving dish. Heat the juices until they start to boil, add the flour and then, with a little water, mix to a paste. Stir for at least three minutes while gradually adding the wine.

FINISHING AND SERVING: Reduce the heat and slowly add the cream while stirring. Pour the sauce over the chicken portions and serve with seasonal vegetables and mashed potatoes made with a little cream, butter and chopped chives. You could also serve this with a crunchy salad and some warm, crusty bread. A light dressing for the salad such as honey and mustard would work well. Try a salad finished with fresh herbs such as pineapple-sage, sorrel or lemon-thyme, or with a few primrose and marigold flowers when available.

Clock Tower Beef

FROM CAIRN O'MOHR WINERY
BY EDITH MOWATT

Clock Tower Beef was created to raise funds for the repair of the clock at Crimmond Church, Aberdeenshire.

Cook's Tip: If you only have set honey, this can be used without any problems. Just place a jar of set honey in hot water (with the lid loosened) and it will become clear honey!

450g/1lb round steak cut into strips
1 onion, chopped
1 carrot, cut into strips
2tbsp olive oil
1tbsp clear honey
150ml/¼ pt chicken stock
150ml/¼ pt Cairn O'Mohr Bramble Wine
1tbsp bramble jelly
Handful fresh brambles
Salt and pepper to season

MAKING: Heat the oil in a pan, add the onion and carrot and gently brown. Remove from the pan and reserve. Add the beef and brown all over. Remove from the pan and set to one side. Deglaze the pan with the wine, scraping the residue from the base, and boil to reduce by half. Add the stock and boil to reduce by half again. Add the bramble jelly, honey and ³/₄ of the fresh brambles, and reduce once more over a high heat.

FINISHING AND SERVING: Return the meat and the vegetables to the pan and coat with the sauce, tasting and adjusting the seasoning if required. Use the remaining fresh brambles as a garnish for the finished dish and serve at once with rice or crusty bread. This recipe also goes well with jacket potatoes. Rub a little salt into the skin of the potatoes before cooking to increase their crispiness. Use potatoes that have little or no marks on the surface and make sure that they are washed before use.

Cod Brandade

FROM CARROLL'S HERITAGE POTATOES
PREPARED BY MARTIN WISHART OF RESTAURANT MARTIN WISHART

Cook's Tips: If using saffron, soak a few strands in a little warm water to release the full flavour and colour. Alternative potatoes that can be used include Red Duke of York, Arran Victory or even Edzell Blue. Each has its own distinct flavour and it is worth trying a few different varieties.

500g/1lb British Queen potatoes	125g/4oz unsalted butter
300g/10oz thick fillet of cod	2tbsp olive oil
125g/4oz coarse sea salt	½ onion
30g/1oz sugar	1 clove garlic
1 clove garlic, sliced	Few sprigs fresh thyme
10 fennel seeds	1pt milk
Pinch saffron (optional)	½ lemon, juiced
1tbsp chopped parsley	

SALTING THE COD: Mix the sugar, salt, sliced garlic, fennel seeds and saffron (if using) in a bowl and sprinkle the mixture evenly over the cod. Cover with clingfilm and refrigerate for six hours. When ready, remove the cod from the salt mix and wash in cold running water for two to three minutes. Place on a towel to dry. The prepared cod can then be stored in the fridge until ready for cooking.

COOKING THE COD: Place the cod in a pan and just cover with milk. Add the ½ onion, thyme and unsliced garlic. Bring to the boil, reduce the heat and simmer for two minutes. Remove from the heat, and allow to stand for a further five minutes. Wash, peel and cut the potatoes into evenly-sized pieces. Cover with warm water, add a pinch of salt and gently simmer until cooked. Drain and allow to dry in a colander. Remove the cod from the milk and flake the flesh into a bowl using your fingers. Add the warm, dry potatoes, chopped parsley, butter and olive oil. Using a fork, gently crush the potatoes and fish, adding the lemon juice, and mix well.

FINISHING AND SERVING: Do not mash the potatoes, but leave a good texture. Serve at once with some fresh toast and a seasonal salad.

Coronation Turkey

FROM GARTMORN FARM

Cook's Tips: This could be served as either a generous starter or as a main course. A few freshly cut chives or curly-leaf parsley over the top just before serving will add to the fresh flavour of the dish.

900g/2lb cooked turkey breast meat, cut into thin strips
1 large onion, sliced
1tbsp medium curry powder
25ml/5tsp of either orange or apple juice
12 dried apricots, chopped
6 dates, chopped
250ml/9fl oz mayonnaise
1tbsp oil
Salt and pepper to season
Chopped apples and sliced cucumber to garnish

MAKING: Heat the oil in a frying pan and gently cook the onion until translucent. Add the curry powder and cook for a further minute, stirring constantly. Add the apple or orange juice and stir together. Transfer to a mixing bowl or food processor. Add half the apricots and blend into a smooth paste, then leave the mixture to cool. When cold, add the remaining apricots, the dates and the mayonnaise together with the sliced cooked turkey meat and mix until well blended.

FINISHING AND SERVING: Season to taste and refrigerate until ready to serve. Turn out into a serving dish and decorate the surface with the garnish of chopped apples and sliced cucumber. Alternatively, serve on a bed of rice – try it with one of the coloured varieties such as camargue red or imperial black. The flavour of the coloured rice is a lot more 'nutty' than the usual white rice and compliments the spiciness of the sauce.

Crimmond Lemon Chicken

FROM CAIRN O'MOHR WINERY
BY EDITH MOWATT

Cook's Tip: Try with a stir-fry of baby sweetcorn, mange tout and batons of carrot.

4 chicken breasts
1tbsp light soy sauce
1 bunch spring onions
5tbsp cornflour
1 lemon, juiced
2tsp sugar
2tbsp Cairn O'Mohr Spring Oak Leaf Wine
1 clove garlic, crushed
150ml/¼ pt chicken stock
4tbsp olive oil
Salt and pepper to taste

MAKING: Wash and dry the chicken and cut into equally-sized strips. Place in a bowl with the soy sauce and toss to coat the chicken. Add 4tbsp of the cornflour to the bowl and mix well. Mix the lemon juice, garlic and sugar in a separate bowl. Make a paste with the remaining cornflour and a little water. Heat the oil in a heavy-based pan, cook the chicken in small batches then remove and set to one side. Add the spring onions to the pan with the garlic mixture and fry for two minutes. Add all of the remaining ingredients except for the cornflour paste and reduce the sauce over a high heat.

FINISHING AND SERVING: Thicken the sauce with the cornflour paste and pour over the reserved cooked chicken. Serve with plain boiled rice or with floury potatoes, boiled and lightly crushed. Steamed broccoli would also go very well with this dish. Put a dash of sesame oil on the broccoli for a different flavour.

Elizabethan Turkey

FROM GARTMORN FARM

The use of a wide variety of spices was very common in Elizabethan times, because it showed off the wealth of the host.

Cook's Tip: This recipe can be adapted for yeast intolerance by using gluten-free flour and apple juice in place of the wine or cider.

1.5kg/3lb turkey thigh meat, diced
2 large onions, sliced
1 head celery, diced
175g/6oz dried apricots, chopped
175g/6oz raisins
1 lemon, juice and zest
1 orange, juice and zest
175g/6oz stoned dates, chopped
2 large apples, chopped
1tsp honey
1tsp plain flour
4tbsp olive oil
½ bottle red wine or cider
1tsp each of the following: cinnamon, mace, black pepper, marjoram, thyme, mild curry powder
3 cloves garlic, crushed
Salt to season
Sliced oranges and toasted walnuts to garnish

Preheat the oven to 160°C/325°F/Gas 3.

MAKING: Heat the olive oil in a pan, coat the turkey meat with the flour and lightly brown. Remove the meat from the pan and transfer to a casserole dish. Fry the onions and celery for two to three minutes and add to the casserole dish. Add the remaining ingredients to the meat, celery and onions, except for the orange and walnut garnish, and season to taste with the salt. Mix well, cover and cook in the middle of the oven for 2½-3 hours or until tender.

FINISHING AND SERVING: Remove from the oven and garnish with the orange slices and toasted walnuts. Serve with rice or with potatoes and seasonal vegetables. Try one of the potato varieties such as Pink Fir Apple for an old-fashioned flavour. Dress the edge of the plates with a sprinkling of paprika for an extra touch.

Fish in Cider

Cook's Tips: Try this with smoked fish, or mix different types of fish. Add a few finely-diced mixed vegetables to the onion, such as three colours of peppers. Use red onions instead of the normal white for a different coloured effect. The alcohol in the cider will evaporate if it is boiled. You could add a little cider vinegar to the sauce if using apple juice, as this may be too sweet.

350g/12oz firm white fish, skinned and cubed
60g/2oz flour
1 small onion or 2 small shallots, chopped
1 clove garlic, crushed
1 egg, beaten
300ml/½ pt dry cider or dry apple juice
Few strands of saffron
Oil for frying

MAKING: Heat the oil in a pan. Dip the cubed fish into the beaten egg and then into the flour. Shake off any excess and place the fish into the hot oil. Fry for about 1-1½ minutes, remove from the oil and keep warm. Add the chopped onion (or shallots), the garlic and the saffron and cook gently until the onion becomes transparent. Add the cider or apple juice, boil for two minutes and then reduce the heat to a simmer.

FINISHING AND SERVING: Return the fish to the pan to heat through and serve at once.

Fresh Scallops Wrapped in Bacon with Basil

Cook's Tips: Use flavoured oil such as garlic or rosemary to infuse an extra taste. Add a strip of smoked salmon under the bacon. Make into kebabs by passing three or four 'parcels' onto a skewer that has been soaked in cold water, and cook under a medium grill or on a barbecue.

Fresh scallops (roe removed) for 4 people
Smoked bacon, cut into strips
Fresh basil leaves

PREPARING: Wrap each scallop with one basil leaf then with a strip of bacon. Secure with a cocktail stick if necessary.

FRYING THE SCALLOPS: Pan fry each 'side' in olive oil for about two minutes until the bacon is cooked and the scallop has browned on each end.

FINISHING AND SERVING: Season with salt and pepper to taste. Serve with fresh warm crusty bread.

Green Omelette

Cook's Tip: Try various herbs to flavour the omelette depending on what is in season. Tarragon, coriander or chives will all work well.

6-8 eggs
2 leeks, washed and chopped
4 spring onions, chopped
110g/4oz spinach, washed and chopped
45ml/3tbsp fresh parsley, chopped
Pinch mixed herbs
1tbsp chopped walnuts or hazelnuts
Salt and pepper

Preheat the oven to 175°C/350°F/Gas 4.

MAKING: Beat the eggs in a large bowl, add all the chopped vegetables, mixed herbs and nuts and season to taste. Pour the mixture into a large, buttered ovenproof dish, cover and bake for 30 minutes. Remove the cover and continue baking for a further 10-15 minutes until the top is coloured.

SERVING: Serve at once. This is a simple lunch for four people, and can be served alongside baked potatoes with a cheese and herb (or sour cream and chive) filling, or with a simple salad and some fresh bread. You can also serve this cold as a sort of frittata.

Green Salad Leaves
with Mustard Dressing

Cook's Tips: You can of course vary the mix of leaves depending on availability and taste. Do not add the ingredients to the oil – rather mix them first, then add the oil. Oil is the carrier for the flavours and does not absorb the flavours of the dressing.

Bunch of mixed green leaves such as lettuce, chicory, rocket,
  endive, watercress, sorrel
¼ small white cabbage, grated
1 small carrot, grated
1 small onion, chopped
45ml/3tbsp olive oil
15ml/1tbsp wine vinegar
5ml/½ tsp coarsegrain mustard
Pinch salt

MAKING: Wash the leaves thoroughly and shred to an even size. Do not cut the leaves, but tear any larger ones. Mix well and add the onion, carrot and cabbage. In a separate bowl, mix together the vinegar, mustard and salt and stir in the oil.

FINISHING AND SERVING: Make sure you add the dressing just before serving and toss well to coat the salad evenly.

Grilled Salmon on Potato Rosti

Cook's Tips: You could add a little chilli powder to the rosti to give it some spice, or try mixing in a little crushed garlic. If you want to keep the rosti in shape, place the potato into a cooking ring in the pan to retain a round, rather than more rustic, shape. Try topping the salmon with some crispy, deep-fried prawns. Simply take some fresh prawns and drop them into hot oil for a few seconds. Top this off with some drops of chilli oil or a drop of oyster sauce for an oriental flavour.

4 x 75g/4oz salmon steaks, skinned
350g/12oz potatoes, coarsely grated
1 small clove garlic, crushed
1 egg, beaten
3tbsp milk
30g/1oz butter
½ lemon, juiced
Salt and pepper to season
Vegetable oil for frying

MAKING: Mix together the egg and milk. Heat the oil in a pan. Place the grated potato into a bowl, add the crushed garlic, egg and milk mix and coat well. Take a handful of potato, form into a rough round then place it in the oil. Cook for about four to six minutes until browned, turn over and repeat. Remove from the oil and drain. In a separate pan, melt the butter. Place the salmon steaks into the hot butter and cook for about three minutes per side or until the salmon is just opaque and cooked, but not dry.

FINISHING AND SERVING: Put one rosti per person onto a serving dish, top with the salmon and pour a little of the juice from the pan over the top. Squeeze a little lemon juice over, season to suit and serve at once with green vegetables.

Hot Arbroath Smokie Creel

FROM IAIN R SPINK, ARBROATH
PREPARED BY KEVIN GRAHAM

Cook's Tips: Use fresh herbs for a better flavour. If you use dried, reduce the quantity as their flavour is in fact stronger. Try using lemon-thyme to increase the intensity of the herb's flavour.

1 pair smokies, boned and skinned
350g/12oz cooked rice, with saffron
$^{1}/_{2}$ onion
50g/2oz mushrooms
15g/$^{1}/_{2}$ oz butter
150ml/$^{1}/_{4}$ pt fresh cream
$^{1}/_{2}$ lemon, juiced
1 measure Vermouth
Pinch fresh thyme
Pinch fresh parsley
Pinch turmeric
$^{1}/_{3}$ pt fish veloute (see below)
12 individual short pastry tart cases

MAKING THE VELOUTE: The veloute is very easy to make. Simply make a roux (or paste) by mixing 3tbsp flour and 2tbsp melted butter in a pan, then add 1$^{1}/_{2}$ cups of boiling fish stock. Mix together, stirring to prevent lumps. Bring to the boil (and if using fresh fish stock, skim off any residue). Add half a dozen crushed peppercorns and continue cooking to reduce the quantity by about $^{1}/_{3}$. Strain and use as below.

MAKING THE CREEL: Finely dice the onion and slice the mushrooms. Flake the smokies and set to one side. Gently heat the butter in a medium pan and sweat the onions, taking care not to brown them. Add the sliced mushrooms and cook gently for a further two minutes. Add the Vermouth and reduce the liquid by half. Add the fish veloute, turmeric, parsley, thyme and lemon juice. Cook for ten minutes and finish the sauce by adding the cream. Check the seasoning, adding salt and pepper if required. Taking care not to re-boil, add the flaked smokies and simmer for five minutes.

FINISHING AND SERVING: Lay the saffron rice onto a warmed serving dish, place the short pastry tart cases on top and spoon the smokie mixture into the cases. Garnish with wedges of lemon and fresh parsley.

Juniper and Garlic Pork Fillet

Cook's Tips: You could use fresh apple juice in place of the cider if preferred, or a dash of cider vinegar to bring a touch of sharpness to the dish. The juniper has a very subtle but distinctive flavour. You may normally see it with venison, but it is versatile and goes well with the pork in this recipe. Try with pork chops in place of the fillet, or use collops or medallions of pork. Chicken also works well, as do rabbit or veal.

1kg/2lb pork fillet
275ml/½ pt dry cider
30ml/2tbsp olive oil
6-8 juniper berries, crushed
2 cloves garlic, crushed
25g/1oz plain flour
Salt and pepper

MAKING: Cut the pork fillet into four pieces and lay them on the base of a shallow, ovenproof dish. Mix together the juniper berries, garlic and olive oil and coat the pork all over. To marinade, cover and leave in a cool place overnight or for a minimum of three hours.

COOKING: When ready to cook, remove the meat and reserve the marinade. Then heat a heavy-based pan and add the reserved marinade. Cook for two minutes and add the pork. Cook over a moderate heat for ten minutes, turning to evenly colour the surface. Remove the meat from the pan and keep warm. Increase the heat and stir the flour into the cooking juices. Add the cider and boil, reducing the liquid slightly and scraping the residue off the base of the pan at the same time.

FINISHING AND SERVING: Return the meat to the pan, coat with the sauce, season to taste and serve.

Leek and Seafood Baked Pasta

Cook's Tips: Use coloured pasta for visual effect. Vary the herbs used or try adding a few chilli flakes. Add some crushed garlic into the leeks and onion/shallots as they cook. The seafood mix can be varied to seasonal flavours. You can also try flaked white fish, adding a touch of turmeric for colour.

2 medium leeks
1 medium onion or 4 small shallots
200g/7oz prawns (shell off) or mussels, or combination seasonal seafood
Olive oil
½ oz fresh basil (or 5g/1tsp dried if fresh unavailable)
Salt and freshly-ground black pepper
170g/6oz 'Long' pasta (fresh if available)

Preheat the oven to 200°C/400°F/Gas 6.

MAKING: Wash and slice the leeks very thinly, including some of the green tops, then finely slice the onion or shallots. Fry both in olive oil for five minutes without browning. Add the seafood and basil, season to taste and cook for a further five minutes. Meanwhile, cook the pasta and drain, seasoning with a little freshly-ground black pepper. Put the seafood and leeks into the pasta and mix well. Lightly oil a small individual mould and fill with the pasta mix, repeating with additional moulds until there is no mixture left. *Note: Use small individual moulds like timbales. Ceramic moulds can be used if metal ones are not available.*

BAKING: Put the moulds into a roasting tray half filled with water and place in the oven. Bake for 15-20 minutes.

FINISHING AND SERVING: Turn the pasta out onto a plate (the top of the pasta should be slightly crispy when ready. If it is still a bit too soft, place under a hot grill to finish) and serve with a crispy salad.

Lemon Lamb

900g/2lb boned leg of lamb or lamb fillet
1 lemon, sliced
30g/1oz butter
275ml/½ pt chicken stock
20ml/1tbsp olive oil
2tsp parsley, chopped
¼ tsp saffron strands
¼ tsp cinnamon
Salt and pepper

MAKING: Heat the butter and oil together in a large pan. Add the lamb and brown evenly all over. Sprinkle on the cinnamon and season to taste with salt and pepper. Add the saffron strands to the chicken stock and pour this over the lamb. Place the lemon slices on top of the lamb. Cover the pan and simmer gently for about 1½ hours or until the meat is tender.

FINISHING AND SERVING: Transfer to a warm serving dish, sprinkle over the parsley and serve at once with plain boiled rice or with fresh bread and a green salad.

Marinated Fillet of Pork

Cook's Tip: If the pork has been sliced thinly rather than into strips, serve as a hot sandwich filling.

350g/12oz fillet pork, with the fatty parts removed
2 cloves garlic
Dash olive oil
1 sprig fresh or dried thyme
1 sprig fresh or dried oregano
Salt and freshly-ground black pepper
Pinch paprika
Pinch cayenne pepper

MAKING: Peel and crush the garlic cloves with a little salt and add the herbs and spices. Put into a bowl with a little freshly-ground black pepper and a dash of olive oil. Cut the pork fillet into evenly-sized pieces. Coat the pork fillet with the marinade and cover with clingfilm. Place in the fridge overnight.

COOKING: Remove from the marinade and cook the pork on a hot griddle plate, turning constantly.

SERVING: Serve hot with a simple salad and warm crusty bread, a garlic and herb bread or crostini. Alternatively, serve over couscous or, as a tapas meal, with some marinated olives and strong cheese.

Minted Salad

Cook's Tips: Add a little grated hard cheese if preferred. A few strips of cured ham or smoked duck can also be added.

1 small gem lettuce, shredded
2 medium carrots, washed and grated
2 sticks celery
1 small apple, peeled and diced
15ml/1tbsp seedless raisins
15ml/1tbsp mayonnaise
5ml/1tsp finely chopped fresh mint
½ lemon, juiced

MAKING: Mix the carrot, celery and raisins in a bowl. Arrange the lettuce on a plate and top with the carrot mixture. Spoon over the mayonnaise and sprinkle on the apple and mint.

FINISHING AND SERVING: Squeeze over the lemon juice and serve at once with a seeded bread or as a side dish to a cold game pie.

Mrs Hamilton's Grilled Lamb Chops

FROM MRS HAMILTON'S BEEF AND LAMB

Cook's Tips: If you like to 'eat off the bone', choose the double loin chops or, alternatively, the valentine chop, which is the same cut but without the bone. Good lamb needs little else in terms of flavouring, as the meat is naturally succulent and full of flavour. To keep the chops moist while grilling, overlap the fat from one to the lean of the next and the melting fat will baste the chops.

2 lamb chops per person
Salt and pepper to season

MAKING: Simply preheat the grill to a high setting, place the chops under the heat and brown on either side. Reduce the heat to a low temperature and allow a further four to five minutes according to taste.

SERVING: Serve, seasoned with just a little salt and pepper, with mashed potatoes in the winter, or with new potatoes with a sprig of mint in the summer. Caramelised carrots are really nice with lamb chops. To cook, simply cut the carrots lengthways into batons and place in a saucepan with a large knob of butter, a generous tablespoon of brown sugar and just a splash of water. Cover the pan, cook for four to five minutes and serve.

Try also with quick-cooked red cabbage. For this, shred the cabbage and place it in a pan with a dash of cider vinegar or white wine vinegar, a dash of water and a few pieces of chopped apple or a few raisins. Cover with a tight-fitting lid and cook for two minutes, shaking the pan to mix the cabbage and liquid. Remove from the heat, drain and serve at once.

Mrs Hamilton's Meat Loaf

FROM MRS HAMILTON'S BEEF AND LAMB

Cook's Tips: Try mutton mince if you cannot get lamb mince. It's cheaper as well! You can use just beef and bacon if you do not like lamb, but remember to make up the quantity of mince. For a spicy taste, add a little cajun spice mix or a few drops of Tabasco or pepper sauce. Add in some fresh herbs, parsley and pine nuts for a further variation. If you double the quantity, the meat loaf is delicious served cold as well – try with a fresh leaf, potato or bean salad. The best breadcrumbs can be made with the heel end of a granary loaf for extra texture.

250g/8oz minced lamb
250g/8oz minced beef
200g/7oz dry cured bacon
2 medium carrots
1 medium onion
75g/3oz fresh breadcrumbs
2tbsp Worcestershire sauce
2tbsp tomato ketchup
Salt and pepper to season

Preheat the oven to 190°C/375°F/Gas 5.

MAKING: Place the minced lamb and beef in a large bowl. Chop the dry cured bacon in a food processor and add to the lamb and beef. Add the fresh breadcrumbs to the meat. In a processor, chop the carrots and onion and add to the bowl, then stir in the Worcestershire sauce and tomato ketchup. Season with salt and pepper and mix together well by hand.

COOKING: Once thoroughly combined, either form into individual bite-size balls and place on a baking sheet OR place the whole mix into a loaf tin. Place the meatballs or loaf into the hot oven. Cook the balls for 45 minutes OR the meatloaf for 1½ hours.

FINISHING AND SERVING: Once cooked through, remove from the oven and serve at once. You could simply serve with plain boiled rice or with fresh bread and a green salad. Otherwise try with boiled potatoes, cauliflower, carrots and a white sauce. Served cold, it goes well sliced in a fresh crusty roll with lettuce and tomato. Alternatively, try hot with pasta and a basic tomato sauce – especially good for the meatballs!

One Pot Fish with Vegetables

This is an easy one-pot fish stew. Vary the vegetables to whatever is in season, but keep the potatoes, as the starch in them will help thicken the liquid.

Cook's Tips: Try with sweetcorn, purple broccoli and red or yellow peppers. Add a small amount of chilli flakes or pepper sauce for a spicy flavour. A squeeze of tomato puree will add a bit of extra colour if desired. For the last five minutes of cooking, put in a few prawns or other shellfish, such as clams or mussels, as well as the fish.

350g/12oz firm white fish, skinned and cubed
2 medium potatoes, chopped
1 medium carrot, chopped
1 small onion, chopped
100g/4oz broccoli, washed and chopped
300ml/½ pt fish stock
300ml/½ pt milk
Salt and pepper to season

MAKING: Put all the ingredients into a large pan. Slowly bring to the boil and cook for ten minutes. Reduce the heat and simmer a further five minutes or until the vegetables are cooked, but not disintegrating.

FINISHING AND SERVING: Season and serve with crusty bread, rice or mashed potatoes to soak up the sauce.

Ostrich and Tomato Stew

FROM KEZIE UK LTD

Cook's Tips: For a variation to this recipe, add 275g/10oz of mushroom soup alongside the potatoes and tomatoes, or use creamed mushrooms added 30 minutes before serving. Use the freshest tomatoes available for the best flavour. A small dash of Worcestershire sauce or balsamic vinegar will bring out the flavour of the ostrich meat in a stew.

Yield: 4-6 servings

750g/1³/₄ lb ostrich stir-fry meat, ie diced steak from Kezie Farm
250ml/¹/₂ pt boiling water
60ml/3fl oz oil
6 medium potatoes, diced
8 tomatoes, peeled and chopped
3 onions, chopped
30g/1oz flour, seasoned with 5ml/1tsp salt
4 cloves
Pinch pepper to taste

MAKING: Cut the ostrich meat into 2cm/1in cubes, coat with the seasoned flour and set to one side. Fry the onion in the oil until transparent and add the cloves, frying for a further minute. Add the ostrich meat to the pan and brown all over. Pour over the boiling water, season to taste, reduce the heat and simmer for one hour. Add the potatoes and tomatoes and continue cooking for a further one hour until the potatoes are cooked and the ostrich meat is tender.

FINISHING AND SERVING: Adjust the seasoning and serve with plain boiled potatoes and seasonal vegetables for a filling meal, or with a seasonal crunchy salad as a lighter option.

Ostrich Lasagne

FROM KEZIE UK LTD

Cook's Tips: You could use alternating layers of green and white pasta sheets, or try with plum tomatoes in a garlic or basil herb sauce. Extra fresh herbs will add a further flavour to the lasagne. Classic basil, rosemary and parsley will all also add to the taste.

Yield: 6 servings

Meat Sauce	Cheese sauce
750g/1³/₄ lb ostrich mince	1L/1³/₄ pt lukewarm milk
410g/14oz plum tomatoes	15g/3tsp cornflour
1 medium onion, diced	100/4oz butter
1 medium carrot, diced	60g/2oz grated parmesan cheese
1 stalk celery, finely chopped	Pinch nutmeg
4 slices ham or cooked bacon,	18 sheets lasagne
finely chopped	50g/2oz grated cheddar cheese
35g/1¹/₂ oz tomato paste	
30g/1oz chopped parsley	
15g/¹/₂ oz oregano	
150ml/¹/₄ pt water	
75ml/1 glass red wine	
15ml/1tbsp olive oil	
2 cloves garlic, crushed	

MAKING THE MEAT SAUCE: Heat the oil in a frying pan, add the onion, carrot, celery and garlic and cook until soft. Add the ostrich mince and cook until the meat is browned all over. Add the wine and boil until it evaporates. Stir in the tomato paste, plum tomatoes and water and mix well. Reduce the heat and simmer for 45 minutes or until the sauce has thickened. When thickened, stir in the chopped ham or cooked bacon and the herbs.

MAKING THE CHEESE SAUCE: Melt the butter in a pan. Remove from the heat and gradually add the cornflour a little at a time to form a smooth paste, stirring to prevent lumps. Return over a low heat and cook for two minutes. Remove from the heat and gradually add the milk, stirring again. Return to the heat, and boil until the mixture thickens. Remove from the heat and add the parmesan cheese and the nutmeg, stirring until smooth.

MAKING THE LASAGNE: Preheat the oven to 175°C/350°F/Gas 4. Grease a shallow square ovenproof dish, large enough to take two sheets of lasagne side by side without overlapping. Add enough cheese sauce to just cover the base of the dish. Place two sheets of lasagne on the sauce then spread a layer of the meat sauce over the top. Repeat the layers, finishing with a layer of the cheese sauce. Sprinkle with the grated cheddar cheese and leave to stand for two hours. Bake for 40-50 minutes until the lasagne is cooked through and the top is golden.

SERVING: Serve with a fresh seasonal salad and crusty bread, warmed in the oven. Add a herb butter to the bread by slicing a few cuts into the top and putting in some butter mixed with crushed garlic. Try mixing thyme, sage or rosemary into the butter as an alternative flavour.

Ostrich Stroganoff

FROM KEZIE UK LTD

Ostrich meat is one of the healthiest options available.

Cook's Tip: If you don't have sour cream to hand, simply add the juice of half a lemon to ordinary cream and leave at room temperature for 30 minutes before using.

Yield: 6 servings (or 4 very generous portions)

1kg/2lb ostrich steak from Kozie Farm
250g/9oz mushrooms, sliced
300ml/½ pt mushroom soup
250ml/⅓ pt sour cream
125ml/¼ pt tomato juice
60g/2oz butter
1 clove garlic, crushed
1tsp pepper
Salt to taste

MAKING: Cut the ostrich steak into 2cm/1in strips and brown in the butter in a medium pan. Add the mushrooms and the tomato juice and stir together. Cover and simmer for 30 minutes. Add all the remaining ingredients, stir well and simmer gently for one hour, stirring occasionally.

SERVING: Serve with plain boiled rice or buttered noodles. Add a warm crusty bread to the dish for a casual dinner party, or serve with a homemade garlic bread. As an alternative, try blending chives, rosemary, tarragon or thyme with either butter or a soft cheese for a topping to the bread.

Pork Chops with Apple and Raisins

This is a tasty old-fashioned German recipe and it goes well with cabbage cooked with caraway seed, diced onion and boiled potatoes.

Cook's Tip: Try with red cabbage, Brussels sprouts when in season or baked stuffed onions.

4 x medium pork chops
3 small green apples
60g/2oz raisins
60g/2oz butter
1tsp sugar

MAKING: Grill the pork chops under a moderate heat, turning to ensure even cooking. Peel and core the apples and cut into thick slices. Melt the butter in a pan, add the apple, raisins and sugar and fry until the edges of the apple are crispy.

FINISHING AND SERVING: Place the chops onto a serving dish and top with the apple and raisin mix. Serve at once.

Pork and Apple with Ginger Jam

FROM THE CRISP HUT
BY MAUREEN WALLACE

Cook's Tips: Add a few chopped prunes as well as the apple pieces. Use a spray oil to fry and crème fraiche in place of the cream to make a virtually fat free dish! You can vary how thick the sauce gets by the amount of reduction. If it gets too thick, remove from the heat and add a little extra stock, then gently reheat to serve.

4 x pork fillets
1 medium apple
250ml/½ pt chicken stock
75ml/3fl oz single cream
Seasoned flour
1tbsp ginger jam
Oil for frying
Salt and freshly-ground black pepper

MAKING: Cut the pork into collops or small slices and coat lightly with the seasoned flour. Peel, core and chop the apple. Heat the oil and fry the pork gently until cooked through. Remove from the pan. Pour the stock into the pan and increase the heat. Bring to the boil and reduce by half, stirring up any 'crusts' from the pork off the bottom of the pan. Add the cream and apple pieces, continuing to stir. Add the ginger jam, stir well and then return the pork to the pan.

FINISHING AND SERVING: Heat for another minute, season and serve. Try over red rice for a nutty flavour, or with a crisp salad and fresh crusty bread.

Pork Cheek Schnitzels

FROM PUDDLEDUB PORK FARM

Pork cheeks regularly feature on the menu at the Gleneagles Hotel, and are a tasty and flavoursome alternative cut of pork.

Cook's Tip: For a fat-free option heat a non-stick frying pan without oil and, when hot, dust the cheeks with a little flour and dry fry for about two to three minutes per side. Press the cheeks down slightly while cooking, remove from the pan and serve.

2 pork cheeks per person
60g/2oz breadcrumbs
60g/2oz plain flour
2tsp water
Salt and pepper to season
Oil for frying

MAKING: Lay each pork cheek between two sheets of clingfilm and flatten slightly either by hand or using a weighted rolling pin to gently 'bash' them. Dip each cheek into the flour, then the water and then the breadcrumbs. Season to taste with salt and pepper. Heat the oil in a shallow pan, with a lid. Lay the cheeks in the oil and fry for two to three minutes per side, with the lid on.

SERVING: Serve at once with a fresh, crisp salad with a light garlic dressing. Otherwise try with saffron rice or jacket potatoes with lots of butter, mayonnaise or cottage cheese and herbs.

MAKING A SAUCE: If you would like to add a sauce, try the following rustic version. Lightly sauté a finely-chopped onion or shallot with one clove of crushed garlic. Add a few chopped, skinned tomatoes, 1/2 tsp salt, some basil, bay leaves and parsley plus 3tbsp of (very) dry red wine. Stir, cover and simmer for about 20 minutes until the sauce thickens. Remove the bay leaves and serve the sauce with the schnitzels.

Pork Cheek and Vegetable Kebabs

FROM PUDDLEDUB PORK FARM

This recipe works over a barbecue, under a grill or on a griddle plate.

Cook's Tips: If using bamboo skewers, soak them for 30 minutes in cold water before assembling the kebabs to prevent the ends of the skewer burning. Run a little oil along the length of each skewer to help ease the portions on. Also, use gloves to turn metal skewers, as they can get very hot.

If you cook on a barbecue, never leave the cooking unattended, and do not use water to cool a high heat, simply lift the food higher from the heat source to adjust the cooking temperature.

2 pork cheeks per person
1 small red pepper
1 small green pepper
2 medium tomatoes
3 small mushrooms
1 medium onions
2tsp olive oil
2tsp honey
Generous pinch mixed fresh herbs of choice
Freshly-ground black pepper

MAKING: Slice each pork cheek into six to eight pieces width-ways. Slice the onion into sections, not rings, then de-seed and slice the peppers into evenly sized pieces. Cut each tomato and mushroom in half. Starting with either, thread alternate vegetables and pork onto a skewer (see *Cook's Tips*) allowing one cheek per skewer, per person. Brush with oil and grill over a high heat for two minutes. Turn, grill for a further minute and turn again, grilling for one more minute. When ready, the vegetables should be very slightly 'charred' and the pork cheeks coloured around the edges. The timing can be increased slightly to get the best appearance, though take care not to dry out the kebabs.

FINISHING AND SERVING: Sprinkle with herbs and freshly-ground black pepper to season, drizzle honey along the length of each kebab and allow to grill for one more minute. Serve kebabs hot. Try with some strong herbs such as lemon-thyme, curry leaf, marjoram or oregano or any seasonal variations that you enjoy. Fresh herbs are best, but dried will work just as well.

Potato Omelette

Cook's Tips: Add a little chopped tomato to the egg and potato mix before cooking the eggs. Garnish with fresh oregano, basil and thyme before cooking the second side. Include a small amount of cooked chicken liver, chopped sausage or crispy bacon pieces for a more substantial meal.

600g/1¼ lb potatoes
6 eggs
1 clove garlic
Olive oil for frying
Salt and freshly-ground black pepper

MAKING: Peel and slice the potatoes and dry on kitchen towel if necessary. Brush the bottom of a deep pan with olive oil, crush the garlic clove and fry the potatoes with the garlic for about 20 minutes. Remove from the pan when tender and drain off the excess oil. Beat the eggs, season and then add the cooked potatoes.

COOKING: Place the mix into a deep heat-proof pan with a little oil over the whole of the base. Cook for about four minutes until the eggs set on the underside. Either place the pan under a grill to cook the top, or carefully turn the omelette over and cook the other side for a further two minutes, or until set. Do not overcook as the omelette should be creamy in the centre.

FINISHING AND SERVING: Transfer to a warm plate, cut into wedges and eat at once.

Rabbit with Mustard and Thyme

Cook's Tips: This recipe works really well with chicken as an alternative, but rabbit is a very healthy option with a similar taste when cooked and is worth trying if you have never had it before. If using chicken, try a couple of different herbs as well, such as chives or sorrel, with a light lemony flavour.

1 rabbit, jointed
30ml/2tbsp mustard powder
30ml/2tbsp plain flour
15ml/1tbsp thyme, chopped
100ml/4fl oz water
Salt and pepper

Preheat the oven to 175°C/350°F/Gas 4.

MAKING: Mix the mustard powder with a little water, then add the flour and chopped thyme and season to taste. Gradually add the water to make a paste, stirring all the time to ensure an even mix. Spread evenly over the jointed rabbit. Place the rabbit on a greased baking tray and cook for 1-1½ hours until tender.

SERVING: Serve hot with baked potatoes and seasonal vegetables. Garnish the finished dish with the same herbs used in the cooking.

Roast Leg of Pork
with Calvados Gravy

Cook's Tips: Resting the meat will make it easier to carve and will result in a better flavour. If you can get extra pork rind, cook this at the same time as the rest of the pork, as extra crackling is always in demand! Salt well and cook in oil in a separate pan to the joint.

4kg/8lb leg of pork
Oil and plenty of salt to rub in the rind for crackling
1tbsp calvados (or ordinary brandy)
2tbsp plain flour
375ml/³/₄ pt chicken stock
125ml/¹/₄ pt unsweetened apple juice

Preheat the oven to 245°C/475°F/Gas 9.

COOKING THE PORK: Score the rind of the pork with a sharp knife in a diamond pattern and rub in oil and salt all over. Place the pork, rind up and uncovered, on a rack in a large pan with a little water in the base. Put into the heated oven and cook for 30 minutes. Reduce the heat to 175°C/350°F/Gas 4 and cook for a further 2 hours and 40 minutes (equivalent to 20 minutes per 500g/1lb). Check the crackling, which should be forming, and cook for a further 30 minutes. The pork is ready if, when pierced, the juice runs clear. Remove from the oven and rest for 10-15 minutes.

MAKING THE GRAVY: Leaving about 2tbsp of the juices in the pan, pour off the rest and put the pan over a moderate heat. Add the calvados and scrape the base of the pan to lift the sediment. Cook for about one minute, remove from the heat and stir in the flour. Stir briskly to prevent any lumps forming and return the pan to the heat. Cook for a further two minutes. Add the stock and apple juice and boil, stirring all the time. Cook for a few minutes more to thicken and reduce slightly.

SERVING: Slice the pork and serve with crackling to one side and the gravy poured over the top. Serve with a fresh apple sauce, green beans and sweet roast potatoes.

Roasted Leg of Lamb

FROM TOMBUIE SMOKEHOUSE
BY SALLY CRYSTAL

Cook's Tips: This lamb is also excellent served cold with warm crusty bread and a fresh seasonal salad. If serving cold, you can omit the making of the sauce and use mint jelly, a curried fruit or apple chutney instead.

Lamb	Sauce
1 leg Tombuie Smoked Lamb	½ pt lamb stock
(bone in or out)	¼ cooking juices from the lamb
Brown breadcrumbs, enough to	2tbsp crème fraiche
cover the leg of lamb	2tsp redcurrant jelly
Chopped mint, dried or fresh	
Cracked or ground black pepper	

Preheat the oven to 190°C/375°F/Gas 5.

MAKING THE LAMB: Mix the breadcrumbs with the mint and pepper. Place the lamb in an ovenproof dish and cover with the seasoned breadcrumbs. Cover the meat with foil and cook for 20 minutes per lb. Remove the foil 15 minutes before the end of the cooking time to allow a crust to form. When cooked, remove the meat from the oven and allow to rest. If serving the lamb hot, reserve ¼ of the juices from cooking to make the sauce.

MAKING THE SAUCE: Put the reserved juices into a pan and add ½ pt of lamb stock, the crème fraiche and the redcurrant jelly. Stir and heat through, reducing slightly. Transfer to a sauceboat.

SERVING: Serve the lamb hot with the sauce, creamy mashed potatoes and seasonal vegetables. (See *Cook's Tips* above if serving cold.)

Salmon Steak with Mustard and Honey Crust

Cook's Tips: Use a flavoured mustard, but make sure it has a coarse-grain texture. Try this with pork fillet steaks or chops, or with a firm white fish steak such as halibut or cod.

4 salmon steaks
4tsp clear honey
3tsp coarsegrain mustard
10ml/2tsp oil for frying
Salt and pepper to season

MAKING: Brush the salmon steaks with a little oil. Mix together the mustard and honey to make a paste. Heat the oil in a heavy-based pan and cook the salmon for about three minutes per side. Coat one cooked side of the salmon with the mixture and place under a grill on a high heat setting for about one minute until the top of the honey and mustard is slightly brown and bubbling.

SERVING: Serve at once with a tasty herb salad with a blue cheese and pear dressing, or with fresh steamed vegetables.

Scallops in Black Pasta with Chilli

Cook's Tips: Always use the freshest scallops available. This recipe will also work well with salmon pieces, king prawns, crab meat or even lobster! The black pasta is simply pasta coloured with squid ink.

Fresh king scallops, including the roe, for 4 people
350g/12oz black pasta linguini or spaghetti
2 red chillies
Salt and freshly-ground black pepper for seasoning
Olive oil

MAKING: Place the pasta into a pan full of boiling water, with a little salt and olive oil. Cook one end of the king scallops on a very hot griddle for about 90 seconds, then turn and cook for a further 60 seconds. De-seed the chillies and chop very finely. Drain the black pasta, season with freshly-ground black pepper and add the chillies.

FINISHING AND SERVING: Add the cooked scallops to the pasta and serve with a little olive oil over the top. For the best effect, serve on a white plate on a black charger. Make a 'crown' of the pasta by using a double-pronged fork to lift the pasta out of the pan, twisting it so that the pasta forms a 'ball', and slip it off onto the plate. It should stay together! Pile the seafood around and enjoy with a crispy salad and fresh crusty bread. A few chives over the pasta also look effective.

Seafood Fishcakes with Leeks

Cook's Tips: Use Japanese breadcrumbs or flakes to coat. These are quite different to the usual crumbs and give a distinctive appearance. Also, put some grated coconut into the crumbs for texture. To cook the potatoes quickly, grate them first and then boil for about seven minutes before mashing. A little chilli in the potato mix adds some extra flavour. Either use chilli flakes or a few drops of chilli oil or sauce.

250g/8oz prawns (shell off), mussels or white fish. This can either
  be cooked in advance or fresh
2 medium leeks
1 small red onion
400g/14oz potatoes, cooked and mashed
1 clove garlic
1 small egg, beaten
10g/1tsp chives, finely chopped
Oil for frying
Flour for coating
Salt and freshly-ground black pepper for seasoning

MAKING: Wash and slice the leeks and the red onion very thinly. Cook them both with the crushed garlic in a little oil for seven to ten minutes without browning. Cook the seafood if fresh and uncooked, either by stir-frying for two to four minutes in a little oil or poaching in some fresh fish or vegetable stock. *Note: Be careful not to overcook the seafood, as it can become quite tough and rubbery in texture if cooked for too long.* Then chop or flake into small pieces. Put the leek and red onion mix plus the chives and seafood into the mashed potato and stir together. Season to taste with salt and pepper.

FINISHING AND SERVING: With your hands, make up four small rounds or cakes, dip into the beaten egg and then into the flour to coat. Shallow fry the cakes for about five minutes per side and serve.

Silverside of Beef with Bramble Wine, Shallots and Tarragon

FROM CAIRN O'MOHR WINERY
BY EDITH MOWATT

Cook's Tip: A little lemon juice added with the zest will enhance the citrus flavour, though be careful not to add too much as the tarragon has a delicate lemony flavour of its own.

6 medallions silverside
8 shallots, peeled
4 whole cloves garlic, peeled
1 whole lemon
450ml/³/₄ pt chicken stock
100ml/3fl oz Cairn O'Mohr Bramble Wine
2tbsp olive oil
2tbsp crème fraiche
2tsp fresh tarragon
Salt and pepper to season

MAKING: Zest the lemon and finely shred the tarragon. Heat the olive oil in a large pan, season the beef with salt and pepper and fry for three minutes per side, or until evenly browned. Remove the beef from the pan, add the shallots and garlic and fry over a moderate heat for five minutes, stirring. Add the lemon zest, tarragon, wine and stock and stir well, scraping the base of the pan to incorporate any bits. Boil the liquid, return the beef to the pan and reduce the heat. Simmer for 15 minutes. Remove the beef from the pan and set aside. Add the crème fraiche to the sauce and stir well.

FINISHING AND SERVING: Boil rapidly to reduce the sauce. Taste and adjust seasoning if required. Pour the sauce over the beef and serve at once. This is perfect with some tasty fresh bread, such as a sunflower seed loaf or a crusty bread made with bran for a lovely rustic texture. To make a more substantial meal try serving with a light boiled rice or with pasta. For a different taste try red rice cooked for 20 minutes in beef stock.

Simple Chicken Taster

Cook's Tip: Add to pasta with soy sauce and a very few chilli flakes, or to coloured rice, such as red, or black and white rice mix, or serve over puy lentils.

500g/1lb 2oz (about 4 medium-sized) chicken breasts, skin removed
1tbsp sesame seeds
110g/3^1/$_2$oz grated Parmesan or Rapesan cheese
Olive oil for frying
Butter for frying

MAKING: Leave the chicken breasts whole or, if preferred, cut into smaller bite-sized pieces. Wash the chicken and roll it in the sesame seeds and grated cheese. When well coated, fry gently in a little hot olive oil and butter for about three to five minutes, or until cooked through.

FINISHING AND SERVING: Remove from the pan, drain and leave to cool slightly. Serve over salad leaves with peanuts and cashews, added for texture and taste. Alternatively, serve as a 'nibble' with crudités and dips, such as houmus (ground chick peas) or tahini (sesame seed paste).

Simple Fishcakes

Cook's Tips: Add some chopped prawns or crabmeat for texture and colour. Dip in Japanese breadcrumbs available from any Chinese supermarket. These are 'flat' and flaky with a slightly different texture to normal breadcrumbs. Add some grated coconut to the breadcrumb mix. If you like a spicy flavour, include a little fresh red chilli, de-seeded and finely chopped.

400g/14oz cooked white fish, trout, salmon – firm fleshed is best
400g/14oz potatoes, peeled, cooked and mashed
75g/3oz breadcrumbs
15g/1tsp fresh parsley or chives
20g/1oz flour seasoned with salt, freshly-ground black pepper and a pinch of paprika
2 eggs
1tbsp milk
Oil for cooking
Butter for cooking

MAKING: Flake and combine the fish pieces in any proportion with twice as much mashed potato. Add a little fresh parsley or chives into the mix. In a separate bowl, beat the eggs into the milk. With floured hands, roll a little of the mix into a small ball between the palms, dip into the milk and egg mixture and then into the breadcrumbs. Cook in a little oil and butter until well browned all over, or deep fry in hot oil.

SERVING: Serve with steamed seasonal vegetables or with a crispy salad of mixed peppers, tomatoes, lettuce and capers.

Smoked Salmon (or Trout) with Scrambled Eggs in Croissants

FROM KINTALINE PLANT AND POULTRY CENTRE

Cook's Tips: You could serve this on warm bagels if preferred, but the croissants have a lovely buttery texture that compliments the eggs. Use the freshest eggs you can for this – free range will give the best results.

50g/2oz flaked smoked salmon (or trout) per person
2 medium eggs per person
2 croissants per person (warmed)
30g/1oz cream cheese
2tsp double cream
10g/½ oz butter
Salt and pepper to season

MAKING: Break the eggs into a bowl and whisk together with the cream, adding salt and pepper to season. Slowly melt the butter in a pan and add the egg mixture. Keep the heat to no higher than a medium setting. Let the liquid settle before passing through the eggs with a wooden spoon, stirring very gently until the eggs are just set – do not overmix or beat. Remove from the heat and add half the smoked salmon (or trout) flakes. Meanwhile spread the cream cheese over the warm croissants. Top with the egg mixture and the rest of the salmon (or trout) flakes.

SERVING: Serve garnished with a little chopped parsley or dill. Finish with some freshly-squeezed lemon juice over the fish.

Tagliatelli with Smoked Salmon

FROM TOMBUIE SMOKEHOUSE
BY SALLY CRYSTAL

Cook's Tips: As alternatives, use smoked bacon in place of the smoked salmon. Try with green spinach tagliatelli for a more colourful version. Many types of fish can be used in this simple pasta dish. Try with tuna, halibut steak, trout, prawns, crab, etc. To retain the best flavour, do not add the fish until the dish is to be served. This dish can also be used as a light otaiter if you adjust the quantities to suit.

225g/8oz tagliatelli
1 small onion, finely chopped
100g/4oz smoked salmon, cut into fine strips
300ml/½ pt fresh cream
2tsp Balsamic dressing
Salt and pepper to season
Olive oil for cooking

MAKING: Cook the tagliatelli as per package instructions until just firm. Cook the onion in olive oil until just transparent and then add the balsamic dressing. Add the cream to the onion and dressing, and heat gently for four to five minutes, being careful not to overcook. Do not allow to boil. Drain the tagliatelli, add the sauce and mix together well, seasoning to taste with salt and pepper.

FINISHING AND SERVING: Add the smoked salmon strips and serve at once with a tasty salad of watercress, spinach and parmesan. A simple balsamic vinegar and Dijon mustard dressing will go well with this.

Tartlet with Smoked Venison and Mushrooms

FROM TOMBUIE SMOKEHOUSE
BY SALLY CRYSTAL

Cook's Tips: Use a combination of wild mushrooms in season. Cook the mushrooms with a little truffle oil to add a more intense mushroom flavour, or flame them with a touch of brandy.

1 x 100g/4oz pack smoked venison from Tombuie Smokehouse
250g/9oz mushrooms
2tbsp crème fraiche
10ml/2tsp olive oil
Prepared short pastry tart cases
Pinch of dried coriander
Medium dry Sherry to taste
Salt and pepper to season

MAKING: Chop the mushrooms and fry in the olive oil, seasoning lightly. Drain the mushrooms and allow to cool. Chop the smoked venison and add to the cooled mushrooms. Mix in the crème fraiche and add a little medium dry sherry. When ready, place a small amount of the mix into each of the short pastry cases.

FINISHING AND SERVING: Season and sprinkle a touch of coriander over each tart to garnish. Serve at once with crusty brown bread or with a seeded loaf. If presenting at a dinner party, try with different fresh herbs as a garnish.

Tomato and Herring Salad

Cook's Tips: Use sun blush tomatoes to increase the tomato flavour and a simple dressing, such as oil and lemon juice with a little cracked pepper, to compliment the flavour of the fish. Add a few slices of anchovy and capers or flaked cooked white fish and add a little mint and some fresh peas.

1 cooked herring, or roll mops
2 tomatoes, washed and chopped
1 small cooked potato, diced
1 small cooked beetroot, diced
1 small cooked carrot, diced
1 gem lettuce, shredded
½ red onion, finely chopped
Fresh parsley, chopped, to garnish
Dressing to suit

MAKING: Flake the herring, removing any bones. Place all the other ingredients in a bowl and mix well. Add the herring flakes or place the salad mixture into a serving dish and place the roll mops around.

FINISHING AND SERVING: Combine with a dressing of your choice (see *Cook's Tips* above for a suggestion), garnish with parsley and serve.

Trout in Oatmeal

FROM DRUMMOND TROUT FARM

Cook's Tips: Trout is an excellent source of Omega 3 oils and, cooked as below, is light, healthy and actually low in calories. Draining the cooking oil and butter helps to add to the crispiness of the dish. For a more substantial meal, serve with new potatoes, creamed carrots and parsnip, or with some creamed potatoes and turnip.

4 trout fillets
50g/2oz butter
50ml/2fl oz milk
Medium oatmeal, to coat the trout
1tbsp vegetable oil
Salt

MAKING: Sprinkle the trout with a little salt, dip in the milk, and coat both sides with the oatmeal, pressing gently. Heat the oil and butter in a pan and fry the trout over a high heat for three to four minutes, turning over constantly.

FINISHING AND SERVING: Drain on a paper towel and serve at once with either a dill sauce or, for real kick, a fresh horseradish sauce! Perfect with a fresh herby salad and some warm crusty bread for a good healthy meal.

Trout with Almonds

FROM DRUMMOND TROUT FARM

Cook's Tips: A little dry sherry in the oil and butter adds to the almond flavour. For a variation on this French dish, try using hazelnuts in place of the almonds. Try serving old-fashioned potato varieties, such as Pink Fir Apple, Rattray, Duke of York Red Skinned or Highland Red, boiled and slightly cooled. The older varieties of potatoes always offer better flavour than those grown for consistency in shape rather than taste.

1 whole trout
75g/3oz butter
75g/3oz sliced almonds
1tbsp vegetable oil
½ lemon, juiced
Salt

MAKING: Wash and pat dry the trout and sprinkle with salt. Heat the oil and butter in a pan and, when just foaming, add the trout. Cook for two minutes per side or until lightly browned, spooning the oil over while cooking. Remove from the pan, drain and keep warm. Add the sliced almonds to the pan and cook in the oil and butter until golden.

FINISHING AND SERVING: Place the trout on a serving dish, squeeze over the lemon juice and spoon over the almonds. Serve immediately with new potatoes and seasonal vegetables. For a lighter meal, try a crunchy salad and, of course, a good chilled white wine! Add a few edible flower petals to the salad for extra colour.

Turkey with Horseradish and Cranberry Sauce

FROM GARTMORN FARM

Cook's Tips: For a different taste, try this with couscous. To add flavour to the couscous, follow the instructions on the packet and cook with stock and finely-chopped vegetables. Put the cooked couscous into a small mould, or just use a teacup, and turn out onto the plate so that it finishes as a little 'tower'. To compliment the flavour of the spices, try with crunchy stir-fried mange tout or some fresh parsnip crisps.

900g/2lb diced turkey thigh meat
2 large onions, sliced
2tsp medium curry powder
1tsp ground ginger
1tsp muscovado sugar
40g/1½oz plain flour
450ml/¾pt stock (chicken or vegetable)
2tbsp Worcestershire sauce
2tbsp horseradish sauce
1tbsp cranberry sauce
Olive oil for frying
Salt and pepper to season

Preheat the oven to 190°C/375°F/Gas 5.

MAKING: Heat the olive oil in a frying pan and lightly brown the turkey meat. Add the onions and cook for a further two or three minutes, stirring occasionally. Add the curry powder, ground ginger, muscovado sugar and flour, mix well and cook for a further minute. Add the stock and bring to the boil, stirring constantly until thickened. Add the Worcestershire sauce, cover and place in the oven for 2-2½ hours or until tender.

FINISHING AND SERVING: Remove from the oven, add the horseradish sauce and the cranberry sauce and season to taste. Transfer to a serving dish. Serve with simple boiled potatoes and fresh seasonal vegetables, lightly steamed. Alternatively, serve over red or puy lentils cooked in chicken stock.

Venison Casserole

FROM MILTON HAUGH FARM SHOP
BY TONY REEVE

This recipe is gluten free. It is ideal for entertaining, as it can be served straight from the oven to the table.

Cook's Tips: Venison is the meat of Red, Fallow and Roe deer and is in season from June to September. As a game meat, it is low in fat and very healthy It also benefits from an olive oil marinade to bring out the best of the flavour. Seasonal vegetables can be added to accompany, or try braised chicory or red cabbage, steamed for two minutes in 1tbsp white wine vinegar and 1tbsp water with 1tsp sugar.

Casserole

1½ kg/2¾ lb boned venison shoulder, cut into 2½ cm pieces
225g/8oz wild chestnut mushrooms, thickly sliced
75g/3oz smoked streaky bacon, chopped
300ml/½ pt beef stock
2 carrots, sliced
2 sticks celery, sliced
2 medium onions, sliced
2tbsp olive oil
1 bouquet garni – tie fresh parsley stalks, a bay leaf, some thyme
    and mint leaves with string to make the bouquet garni
2tsp cornflour, diluted with a little water

Marinade

225ml/8fl oz red wine
75ml/3fl oz white wine vinegar
2tbsp olive oil
2tbsp Nicoll's of Strathmore Port Wine Jelly
1 medium onion, grated
1 small carrot, chopped
1 stick celery, chopped
4-5 juniper berries, crushed
1tsp dried thyme
Pinch allspice
Salt and pepper

MAKING THE MARINADE: Warm the olive oil, Strathmore Port Wine Jelly and white wine vinegar and stir until the jelly has melted. Stir in the remaining ingredients, seasoning to taste with salt and pepper. Place the venison dice into a glass bowl and pour over the marinade. Cover and place in the fridge for 12 hours.

MAKING THE CASSEROLE: Preheat the oven to 175°C/350°F/Gas 4. Drain the meat into a colander, reserving the marinade. Strain the marinade through a sieve and set to one side. Heat the oil in a pan and fry the venison in batches to brown all over. Remove the venison from the pan and put it into a casserole dish. Fry the bacon, onions, carrots and celery in the same pan until just beginning to colour and add to the meat in the casserole dish. Pour the reserved, strained marinade over the meat and vegetables and add the stock, mushrooms and bouquet garni. Cover and bake for 2¼-2½ hours. Remove from the oven, stir in the diluted cornflour to thicken and mix well. If the sauce is too thick, add a little boiling water to achieve the desired consistency.

SERVING: Serve with creamy mashed potatoes, sugar-glazed baby carrots and lightly braised cabbage. A good quality port wine Jelly such as Nicoll's of Strathmore is the ideal accompaniment. Try warming the jelly very slightly just before serving to enhance the flavour. The casserole will keep in the fridge for up to three days and is also suitable for freezing. *Note: Allow to cool completely before placing the casserole in either the fridge or the freezer. For smaller portions, transfer the cooked casserole into suitable individual containers before freezing.*

Venison Sausages Casserole

FROM TOMBUIE SMOKEHOUSE
BY SALLY CRYSTAL

Cook's Tips: Venison is a splendid, healthy alternative to lamb or beef and is naturally low in fat and very versatile to use. The lack of fat in the meat means that it can dry out in the cooking process, so be careful not to overcook it. To test if the meat is cooked, press it with the edge of a knife. If the juices are slightly red in colour this indicates that the meat is ready to serve. Try this recipe with venison collops as an alternative by frying the collops in a little oil to sear them first, then adding them to the casserole. Reduce the cooking time to 15 minutes. Try adding a little port to make the sauce slightly stronger in flavour.

Yield: 4 servings

1 pack 10 venison sausages from Tombuie Smokehouse
3 medium carrots, chopped
2 medium onions, sliced
300ml/½ pt stock, made from venison if available, or use lamb
1tbsp oil
1tbsp crème fraiche
2tsp Dijon mustard
1tsp redcurrant jelly
Salt and pepper to season

Preheat the oven to 175°C/350°F/Gas 4.

MAKING: Braise the onions and carrots in a little oil in a pan. Cut up the venison sausages and add to the vegetables. Pour in the stock and stir in the redcurrant jelly, crème fraiche and mustard. Season to taste and transfer to a casserole dish. Cook for one hour and serve.

SERVING: Serve with a celeriac mash or potatoes mashed with the skin left on. Alternatively, try parsnips roasted with honey or brown sugar (which brings out the sweetness) or carrots baked in a little orange juice and brown sugar, cooked in the oven at 175°C/350°F/Gas 4 for 45 minutes.

Venison Shepherds Pie

FROM TOMBUIE SMOKEHOUSE
BY SALLY CRYSTAL

Cook's Tip: Top the potatoes with a little grated cheese and, for a crisp topping, place under a grill until the cheese melts.

1kg/2lb minced venison from Tombuie Smokehouse
1 large onion, diced
440g/1lb mashed potatoes
4 carrots, diced
2 sticks celery, diced
1 small clove garlic, crushed (optional)
40ml/2fl oz olive oil
Stock to cover, ie tinned tomatoes, red wine, tomato juice,
    meat stock/stock cube or combination of the above
A few crushed juniper berries
Pinch thyme
Salt and pepper to season

MAKING: Heat the olive oil in a pan and fry the onion until just coloured. Then add the other vegetables (and garlic if using) and fry for five minutes. In a separate pan, brown the venison then add the cooked vegetables to the meat and mix well. Pour over the liquid stock, add the crushed juniper berries and thyme, season to taste and simmer gently for one hour.

FINISHING AND SERVING: Transfer to a deep dish, top with the mashed potatoes and serve with a few seasonal vegetables such as Brussels sprouts, braised cabbage or chicory. Garnish the pie with chopped chives for presentation. Pipe the mashed potatoes onto the pie with a broad-nozzled piping bag for a special visual effect.

Warming Beef Stew

FROM SPEYSIDE ORGANICS
BY CELIA FRASER

Cook's Tips: If you use dried herbs, reduce the amount, as they have a stronger flavour than fresh herbs. The wine used in the stew should be of good quality: if you wouldn't be happy drinking it, do not use it for cooking! The unused portion from the recipe should accompany the stew as the preferred drink. Vary the vegetables according to taste. Try with fresh broad beans, roast marrow or courgettes, kale or baked beetroot.

500g/1lb 2oz braising steak
200g/7oz mixed dried beans
300ml/½ pt boiling water
415g/14oz tin chopped tomatoes
4 carrots, skinned and roughly chopped
1 onion, chopped
1 cup red wine
2 cloves of garlic, finely chopped
2 red chillies, finely chopped
2tbsp olive oil
1 stock cube
Pinch fresh herbs of choice, eg rosemary, thyme, oregano and marjoram
Salt and pepper to season

STOVE TOP METHOD: In a large pan, heat the olive oil and brown the braising steak all over. Remove from heat and keep warm. In the same pan, add the onion, garlic and chillies and fry for one minute. Add the carrots and return the meat to the pan, with any residual juices. Add the chopped tomatoes and boiling water and crumble the stock cube into the pan, mixing well. Season to taste, cover and simmer for 45 minutes. Meanwhile, boil the dried beans in 600ml/1pt of water. Drain, add more boiling water and cook for 30 minutes or until soft. Add the beans and the cup of red wine to the stew ten minutes before serving and stir well before transferring to a serving dish.

OVEN METHOD: Preheat the oven to 200°C/400°F/Gas 6. Repeat the above preparation. Transfer the stew to an ovenproof casserole dish, cover and bake in the oven for one hour. Prepare the beans as above and stir then into the stew along with the red wine. Cover and cook for a further 30 minutes.

SERVING: Serve at once with boiled potatoes and seasonal vegetables, or with warm garlic bread.

Well Hung and Tender BBQ Brisket

FROM WELL HUNG AND TENDER
BY SARAH MACPHERSON

Brisket is an economically-priced cut of beef but full of flavour. The slow cooking brings out the whole flavour of the meat and the combination of the BBQ sauce and the spiciness of the chilli is perfect for a tasty dinner-party recipe.

Cook's Tips: Be careful when handling fresh jalapeño peppers – they are one of the hottest chillies around. The natural oils in the pepper can irritate and burn, and it is recommended that you rinse your hands after preparing them. If you remove the seeds from the pepper before adding to the stew, it will reduce the intensity of the chilli.

1½ kg/2¾ lb beef brisket from Well Hung and Tender
1 medium onion, chopped
3 cloves garlic, crushed
1 jalapeño pepper, minced, OR 1 jar 'Seeds of Change' organic pasta sauce
　　with jalapeño peppers
1 bottle HP Smoked BBQ Sauce
¼ cup white wine vinegar
¼ cup Worcestershire sauce
2tbsp brown sugar
1tbsp oil
2 level tsp salt
1 level tsp freshly-ground pepper

Preheat the oven to 160°C/325°F/Gas 3.

MAKING: Rub half the salt and pepper all over the brisket and, in a large pan, heat the oil and sear the whole surface of the meat. Reduce the heat and add enough water to cover the meat. Add the onion, garlic and jalapeño pepper (or sauce if using) and bring to the boil. Reduce heat and simmer for two hours. Transfer the meat to an ovenproof dish when ready and reserve the liquid. Combine the HP BBQ Sauce, white wine vinegar, Worcestershire sauce, brown sugar and salt, and pour over the meat in the dish. Cover and bake for four hours. Remove the brisket from the oven and let it stand for 15 minutes. Meanwhile, place the reserved liquid in a pan and reduce to a thick consistency over a high heat. Pour into a suitable jug and reserve.

FINISHING AND SERVING: Slice the cooked meat then serve on a platter with the sauce from cooking and the pepper sauce. Accompany this hearty stew with jacket potatoes topped with sour cream and chives. It is also delicious with boiled rice, as an alternative. Try cooking the rice in beef stock rather than water. Add a few dried chilli flakes, finely-diced carrots and shallots to the cooking water to spice up the rice and to add colour.

Wild Boar with Bouvrage

FROM ELLA DRINKS LTD

Cook's Tips: Wild boar is a meat that matures very slowly and benefits from a slow cooking process to bring out the best flavour. This also ensures that the meat is tender. Try the recipe with pork, lamb or venison as well. All game meats benefit from a slow cooking process, and the same applies for good quality pork. To enrich the dish, take a little of the cooking liquor, place it in a pan over a medium heat and stir in a dash of cream.

Marinade

250ml/½ pt Bouvrage raspberry drink
2tbsp balsamic vinegar
2 cloves garlic, crushed
1tsp ground cumin
Salt and black pepper to season

500g/1lb 2oz wild boar meat
(diced shoulder or similar)
2 medium carrots, sliced
2 medium onions, diced
1tbsp olive oil
1tsp flour

MAKING: Combine the marinade ingredients in a large dish, add the meat and allow to stand overnight. Drain the meat, reserving the liquid. Heat the olive oil in an ovenproof dish and sear the meat to brown it all over. Add the vegetables and the flour. Then add the reserved liquid and bring to the boil, stirring constantly to prevent lumps in the sauce. Season to taste. Remove from the heat, cover and place in an oven at 150°C/300°F/Gas 2 for a minimum of 1½ hours.

FINISHING AND SERVING: Transfer to a serving dish and serve with a simple accompaniment such as boiled rice or mashed potatoes. Creamed celeriac or 'bashed neeps' – mashed turnip – and sweet baby Brussels sprouts would also work well with this. Accompany with a glass of chilled Bouvrage. Bouvrage is a delicious real raspberry juice soft drink that compliments the dark flavour of the game.

Baked Beetroot

FROM THISSELCOCKRIG FARM

Cook's Tip: The beetroot can also be roasted. Bake for two to three hours in a moderate oven – 175°C/350°F/Gas 4 – and allow to cool before removing the skin.

Note: Cooking beetroot is worth the effort, but the beet will release a fairly strong smell while cooking.

1 medium-sized fresh beetroot
125ml/¼ pt sour cream
Chopped chives

MAKING: Trim off any leaves from the beet and place in a large pan of boiling water. Boil for a minimum of one hour or until the skin is easily removed. Remove from the water and allow to cool. Remove the skin by rubbing off with the blunt side of a knife.

FINISHING AND SERVING: Cut the beetroot into wedges and serve with sour cream mixed with fresh chives. When cold, you can also try serving as a side dish in small cubes or slices. Alternatively, try serving hot with a reduction of red wine, bramble jelly and butter.

Cheese and Potato Fried Bites

Cook's Tip: Use a Japanese breadcrumb for a more flaky appearance.

2 medium potatoes, washed and skin on
75g/2½oz white breadcrumbs
60g/2oz strong Italian cheese powder
1½tsp curry powder
2 eggs, beaten
Salt and pepper to season
Oil for deep-frying

MAKING: Slice each potato into 3mm/¼in slices. Cook the slices in a large pan of boiling water for about six to eight minutes, remove from the pan and drain well. Mix together the cheese powder, breadcrumbs and curry, and season. Dip the potato into the beaten eggs and then into the breadcrumb mix. Deep fry the slices until golden and crispy and drain thoroughly.

SERVING: Serve while still warm with a dip such as sour cream and chive, garlic mayonnaise or thousand island. To make an easy thousand island dip, take some fresh mayonnaise (or from a jar), add some tomato puree, a dash of Worcester sauce, a little Tabasco, salt and pepper and mix well. You could use this dip as a base for a good prawn cocktail as well. Simply mix in fresh prawns and serve over shredded salad leaves.

Mixed Vegetables with Herbs

Cook's Tips: This is an easy stovetop way of cooking the vegetables, but you can also roast them. Place all the prepared vegetables of choice and the garlic into a roasting pan and drizzle the olive oil over the top. Sprinkle on the herbs and roast at 175°C/350°F/Gas 4 for 25 minutes, turning occasionally for even cooking. Vary the vegetables used according to the season, or try with parsnips, pumpkin, marrow, squash, carrots and potatoes.

225g/8oz potatoes
225g/8oz courgettes
225g/8oz green pepper
225g/8oz onion
110g/4oz marrow or squash
110ml/4fl oz olive oil
1 lemon, juiced
2 cloves garlic, chopped
Pinch mixed herbs
Salt and pepper to season

MAKING: Prepare all the vegetables by cutting to approximately the same size for even cooking. Place in a large pan and sauté in the olive oil with the garlic and herbs. Add the lemon juice and cook gently for about 30 minutes, stirring occasionally to prevent the vegetables sticking to the base of the pan.

FINISHING AND SERVING: Season and serve at once.

New Potatoes with Lemon

This is based on a Spanish tapas recipe. It can be served cold as well as hot if preferred.

Cook's Tips: The lemon juice can be changed to orange for a variation. There is no need to peel the potatoes, but do wash them thoroughly. If the potatoes appear a little too dry, add a little butter to the pan after draining them and swirl the pan around to coat the potatoes.

675g/1½ lb new potatoes
45g/1½ oz butter
1tbsp lemon juice
1 lemon, zest
Pinch fresh parsley or coriander leaf
Salt and pepper to season

MAKING: Cook the potatoes in a pan of boiling water until just tender. Melt the butter in a small pan, add the lemon juice and warm through gently. Drain the cooked potatoes and place in a large bowl. Pour over the butter and lemon juice.

FINISHING AND SERVING: Sprinkle over the herbs and season to taste and serve at once. Garnish with the zest of the fruit or try some curls of the rind.

Parsnips with Blue Cheese Sauce

Cook's Tips: This sauce goes equally well with fennel, potato, braised celery, cauliflower or even tomatoes. Prepare the various vegetables before pouring over the sauce. Serve as a side dish with rice or potatoes as accompaniments to a main course.

4-6 medium parsnips, washed, peeled and quartered
75g/3oz good quality soft blue cheese, crumbled
25g/1oz butter
25g/1oz plain flour
275ml/¹/₂ pt milk
15ml/1tbsp plain yoghurt
Generous pinch black pepper

PREPARING THE PARSNIPS: Boil the parsnips until tender in a large pan of salted water, drain and set to one side.

MAKING THE SAUCE: Melt the butter in a pan and add the flour to make a roux. Cook for two minutes, stirring constantly to prevent burning. Very gradually, add the milk to make a paste and stir again until smooth. Simmer for two minutes. Add the grated soft blue cheese and black pepper and mix well. Do not allow the sauce to boil. Stir in the yoghurt and cook for a further three to four minutes, stirring all the time.

FINISHING AND SERVING: Place the parsnips in a serving dish and cover with the sauce. Garnish with a sprig of parsley and serve at once.

Potato Dauphinois
with Smokey Bacon

Cook's Tips: This is quite a substantial dish, so be careful not to overload a plate! Try it with a smoked garlic for a different taste, or with different sorts of smoked meat, such as chicken, duck, rabbit, venison, ostrich or wild boar, in place of the crispy bacon pieces.

575g/1lb good firm potatoes
30g/1oz butter
1 clove garlic, crushed
1 onion, finely sliced
100g/4oz strong or mature hard cheese, grated
300ml/$^{1}/_{2}$ pt fresh double cream
6 rashers smokey bacon, cooked until crispy and finely chopped
Salt and pepper to season

MAKING: Lightly grease the sides and base of a shallow ovenproof dish. Slice the potatoes thickly, leaving the skin on. Place a single layer of potatoes in the dish, spread over the butter, then sprinkle the crushed garlic and half of the chopped bacon, cheese and onion over the top. Add a second layer of potatoes and finish with the rest of the bacon, cheese and onion. Pour over the cream, season to taste with salt and pepper and cook in the top of the oven at 175°C/350°F/Gas 4 for about one hour or until the top is brown and the potatoes are cooked through.

SERVING: This is a good accompaniment to stews and casseroles, or used as a base for simply-grilled lamb or pork chops.

Roast Potatoes
with Parmesan and Bacon

Cook's Tip: For a really special flavour, use goose fat in place of the oil.

6 potatoes, peeled
60g/2oz Parmesan cheese, grated
4 rashers smoked bacon, cut into strips
1tbsp rosemary
Oil for roasting
Salt

Preheat the oven to 200°C/400°F/Gas 6.

MAKING: Pour a little oil into a roasting tin and place in the hot oven for ten minutes. Parboil the potatoes in plenty of boiling, salty water for ten minutes, then cut them in half. Mix the grated cheese and rosemary and roll the potato pieces in the mixture. Place the potatoes into the roasting tin in the hot oil and bake for 30 minutes. Remove from the oven and sprinkle the bacon slices on top of the potatoes. Return the pan to the oven and cook for a further 15 minutes or until the bacon and the potatoes are fully cooked.

FINISHING AND SERVING: Remove from the pan, drain and serve hot.

Slow-fried Pink Fir Apple Potatoes with a Semi-soft Cheese

FROM CARROLL'S HERITAGE POTATOES

Pink Fir Apple potatoes are a delicious variety with a nice nutty flavour and a smooth texture.

Cook's Tips: This recipe is suitable for vegetarians. If you place the pan under a preheated grill, you can brown the surface a little if preferred.

500g/1lb Pink Fir Apple potatoes
1 medium onion, thinly sliced
2 cloves garlic
Few sprigs rosemary
110g/4oz Annick Cheese or similar semi-soft cheese
1tbsp oil
1 knob butter
Salt and pepper to season

MAKING: Slice the potatoes to about 3mm/⅛ in thick. Heat the oil and butter in a large frying pan that has a lid. Add the onions and gently fry until soft and slightly coloured. Add the potatoes, garlic and rosemary leaves and season to suit. Toss the pan to coat everything in the oil. Cover and reduce the heat to cook slowly for 20-30 minutes. Stir the pan regularly to prevent the bottom from burning. Slice the cheese thinly and place over the top of the potatoes.

FINISHING AND SERVING: Turn off the heat, cover the pan and allow the cheese to melt into the potatoes. Serve at once, sprinkling a few extra herbs over the surface for added flavour. This would be a great accompaniment for most meats, especially lamb dishes. It would also be an ideal dish to serve at the table, straight from the pan, especially if entertaining outdoors.

Stir-fried Brussels Sprouts
with Sesame Oil

Cook's Tips: Sprouts are an excellent vegetable and are a great accompaniment to many dishes. As a variation to the recipe, add a few cooked horse chestnuts when sautéing the sprouts. If you buy your sprouts on the stalk, slice the stalks very finely and add to the pan as well, as it has lots of flavour in its own right.

300g/11oz Brussels sprouts
10ml/1tbsp good quality vegetable oil for frying
5ml/1tsp sesame oil
1tsp Sesame seeds

MAKING: Wash the Brussels sprouts, peel off the outer leaves and cut the sprouts in half. Heat a wok or large frying pan. Put the vegetable oil into the wok and heat, then place the Brussels sprouts into the hot oil and quickly stir fry for about three minutes. Add the sesame oil and coat the Brussels sprouts.

FINISHING AND SERVING: Add the sesame seeds, remove from the heat and serve.

Stuffed Cucumber

Duxelle is equal quantities of finely-diced mushrooms and onions that are cooked in butter. It can be used as stuffing for a number of dishes, such as: chicken supremes or fillets, pigeon, rabbit, pork, vegetable dishes, omelettes or crepes. *Note: The quantity of ingredients will depend on what you wish to stuff with the duxelle, but should remain equal.* To make it, fry the onions in a little butter until clear and then add the mushrooms. Cook until dry.

Cook's Tips: To increase the volume of the duxelle and vary the flavour, mix in some fine breadcrumbs and herbs. Simply add the breadcrumbs and herbs of your choice to the cooked onion and mushroom mix, heat through and remove to a warm place until required. You can also make the duxelle ahead of time and freeze it until needed. Cover with buttered greaseproof paper before freezing and use within three months.

1 cucumber, about 350g/³/₄ lb
60ml/¹/₈ pt fresh cream
120g/4oz herb and breadcrumb duxelle (see *Introduction* and *Cook's Tips* above)
15g/1oz Parmesan cheese, grated
15g/1oz butter

MAKING: Peel the cucumber and cut into four equal lengths of about 4cm/2in. Remove the centre seeds with a teaspoon, blanch for a few seconds in boiling water, drain and refresh in cold water. Pour the fresh cream over the cucumber, heat the duxelle and place it carefully in the groove in the cucumber. Melt the butter and brush the top of the stuffed cucumber. Sprinkle on the grated cheese and brown lightly under a hot grill.

FINISHING AND SERVING: Garnish with a little chopped parsley and serve hot.

Stuffed Mushrooms

Cook's Tips: Add a few chilli flakes to the breadcrumb mix for an extra-spicy taste. Vary the herbs according to the season. Try rosemary, marjoram, sage, sorrel, thyme, oregano or basil in any combination, to your taste. This recipe can be prepared ahead of time, chilled and cooked when required.

12 large mushrooms
3 large tomatoes
120g/4oz breadcrumbs
50g/2oz butter
2tsp mixed herbs
50g/2oz oats
4tbsp stock or water
10ml/1tbsp olive oil
Salt and pepper to season

Preheat the oven to 175°C/350°F/Gas 4.

MAKING: Peel the mushrooms then remove and chop the mushroom stalks. In a little olive oil, fry the breadcrumbs with the mixed herbs, oats and mushroom stalks, seasoning to taste. Brush the mushrooms with butter and place the mixture into the cups of the mushrooms. Put the stock or water in a dish, then add the filled mushrooms, place in the oven and cook for 20 minutes. Meanwhile, slice the tomatoes in half and grill.

FINISHING AND SERVING: Place the cooked tomato halves on a serving dish and top with the cooked mushrooms. Serve at once with thick-cut slices of crusty bread.

Apple and Spring Oak Tart

FROM CAIRN O'MOHR WINERY
BY EDITH MOWATT

Cook's Tips: Add a few hazelnuts into the nut base for variation. The same mix can also be served in individual glasses. For this, place some of the nut crust into a serving glass after cooking, top with apple puree and then the syllabub, in the same manner as below. A syllabub is a very simple and old-fashioned dessert, said to be the favourite of King Henry VIII. Try the recipe with variations of the puree topping, such as pear halves poached in Spring Oak Leaf Wine and arranged in a ring on the nut crust, or even strawberries poached in wine and served in the same way.

700g/1³/₄ lb cooking apples, peeled and chopped
175g/6oz walnuts
50g/2oz brown sugar
30g/1oz white sugar
30g/1oz butter
225ml/8fl oz fresh cream
50ml/10tsp water
100ml/4fl oz Cairn O'Mohr Spring Oak Leaf Wine
15g/1oz caster sugar

Preheat the oven to 215°C/425°F/Gas 7.

MAKING: Place the apples, white sugar and water in a medium-sized pan and cook until the apples soften. Pass through a sieve to make a puree and set aside. In a processor, make a nut crust by blending the walnuts, brown sugar and butter. Put the nut mixture in the base of a well-greased flan dish and bake for five minutes. Turn the apple puree onto the crust and allow to cool.

FINISHING AND SERVING: Whip the cream, wine and caster sugar together to make a syllabub and spoon over the flan. Serve at once. Garnish the top of the flan with some dried apple rings and mint leaves. Dust the top with a little cinnamon.

Apple Water Ice

FROM LANCHESTER FRUIT
BY DOTTY BENSON

Cook's Tip: Frost the mint leaves by dipping into egg white and then icing sugar.

350g/12oz sliced apple, cored and peeled
225g/8oz sugar
150ml/¼ pt water
2 lemons, juiced
2 oranges, juiced

MAKING: Place the sugar and water in a small pan and dissolve the sugar over a low heat. Bring slowly to the boil and then, when at temperature, keep at a fast boil for one minute. Allow to cool. Cook the apples by gently heating in a pan with 600ml/1pt of water and 1tbsp sugar until soft. Sieve the cooked apples and add the lemon and orange juice. Stir the prepared sugar syrup into the sieved apples, pour into a suitable container and place in the freezer for four hours.

FINISHING AND SERVING: Transfer to the fridge 30 minutes before serving. Turn over with a metal spoon a few times before pouring into chilled glasses or a serving bowl. Serve this fresh refreshing dessert with a few crisp butter biscuits or 'langues du chat'. Make your own with 60g/2oz soft flour, 60g/2oz butter, 90g/3oz icing sugar, two egg whites and a little vanilla essence. Cream the butter and sugar and slowly add the egg whites one at a time. Fold in the flour and vanilla and pipe onto a greased baking sheet with a narrow nozzle. Bake in a hot oven at 200°C/400°F/Gas 6 until light gold and crisp. Garnish the water ice with the zest of both orange and lemon and a sprig of fresh mint. If serving in individual glasses, dip the edges of the glasses in egg white and then into white or coloured sugar to decorate and hang a thin slice of apple from the rim. Fresh strawberries, raspberries or redcurrants add a splash of colour to the presentation of the dessert if you are serving a platter to guests.

Baked Apples
with Raisins and Walnuts

Cook's Tip: To vary the filling, add a few chopped apricots, dates or cherries in place of the raisins and a little spoonful of honey to the fruit mix.

Quantity per person:

1 large cooking apple per person, washed and cored
15g/½ oz Demerara sugar
15g/½ oz soft brown sugar
15g/½ oz unsalted butter
Handful crushed walnuts
Few raisins, chopped
Water

Preheat the oven to 175°C/350°F/Gas 4.

MAKING: With a sharp knife cut just through the skin of each apple about ⅔ of the way up from the base and stand in an ovenproof dish. Cream the butter with the soft brown sugar and add the chopped raisins and a few of the crushed walnuts. Fill the core of the apples with this mixture and sprinkle each apple with the Demerara sugar. Put two or three tablespoons of water per apple in the base of the dish. Bake for about 45 minutes or until the apples are soft in the centre.

FINISHING AND SERVING: Remove from the oven and allow to cool for a couple of minutes. Serve with custard or cream or, for a special treat, drizzle over a little calvados or orange liqueur before serving. Also try sprinkling over a little nutmeg.

Bouvrage Cranachan

FROM ELLA DRINKS LTD

Bouvrage is a soft drink made with the juice of real raspberries.

Cook's Tip: If you don't mind breaking with tradition, add a little grated chocolate as a garnish, or put a few little pieces of diced orange and raspberry into the cranachan to enhance the fruit flavour of the Bouvrage.

250ml/½ pt Bouvrage raspberry drink
100g/4oz medium oatmeal
4tbsp thick heather honey
4tbsp clear honey
100g/4oz cream cheese
150ml/¼ pt fresh double cream + 10ml/2tsp fresh double cream to finish

MAKING: Add the oatmeal to the thick heather honey in a bowl. Add 75ml/⅛ pt of the Bouvrage and allow to marinade overnight. Mix the cream cheese and the remainder of the Bouvrage with the oatmeal and thick heather honey marinade. Beat 150ml/¼ pt of double cream until stiff, and pour into two tall glasses. Then, pour the oatmeal mixture over the beaten cream, and top off with the remaining double cream.

FINISHING AND SERVING: Make a well in the centre, pour in the clear honey and serve.

Lemon Curd Ice Cream

FROM ROSE COTTAGE COUNTRY KITCHEN

A rich dairy ice cream made in minutes, based on an original recipe from 'The Great British Kitchen'.

Note: Use the ice cream within three weeks of making.

600ml/1pt extra thick double cream
400g/14oz (fresh) lemon curd
2 tbsp milk

MAKING: In a large bowl, slowly combine all the ingredients using a hand whisk. When thoroughly mixed, spoon into a container and freeze until required.

SERVING: Remove the ice cream from the freezer 15 minutes before serving and try alongside a nice light accompaniment such as 'langues du chat' biscuits, ratafia biscuits or brandy snaps.

Add lemon juice.

Plum and Hazelnut Crumble

Cook's Tips: Vary the fruit used in the one crumble for additional flavour combinations. Crumbles are a great way to use up the 'ends' of any fruit, so try rhubarb pieces, peaches, apple, or any additional seasonal fruits you may have in the kitchen. *Note: Do not use spoiled or damaged fruit.* Add a little ginger powder to the stewed fruit if desired – a classic combination with rhubarb.

500g/1lb 2oz plums, washed, chopped and lightly stewed
200g/8oz plain flour
100g/4oz butter, chilled
100g/4oz Demerara sugar
50g/2oz roasted hazelnuts, chopped
Whipped cream to serve

Preheat the oven to 190°C/375°F/Gas 5.

MAKING: Sift the flour into a bowl, grate in the butter and mix well. Stir in the sugar and the nuts. Place the cooked plums in an ovenproof dish and top with the crumble mix. Place in the oven and bake for 45 minutes or until the topping is crisp.

SERVING: Serve either hot or cold with plenty of whipped cream, custard or crème anglaise. Crème fraiche is a healthy alternative to whipped cream.

Poached Pears and Stilton Pastry

FROM CAIRN O'MOHR WINERY
BY EDITH MOWATT

Cook's Tips: To really show this dish off, make a spun sugar basket to sit on top of the pear. This is made by boiling a little caster sugar in a pan until it liquefies, but before it can turn completely to caramel, remove from the heat. Dip a metal fork into the sugar and vigorously 'flick' the runny strands over the handle of a wooden spoon. As the sugar cools instantly, the flicking causes it to set as fine strands, which can be gathered and 'rolled' to make a decoration. Place a piece of paper under the handle of the spoon to catch the unused sugar strands. *Note: It is a good idea to practice this beforehand in order to get used to the action required but, once tried a few times, the effect is very grand and can be used to garnish any number of desserts.*

4 fresh pears
60g sugar
50g Stilton cheese
1 lemon, juice and zest
150ml/¼ pt Cairn O'Mohr Strawberry or Raspberry wine
150ml/¼ pt water
¼ stick cinnamon
4 puff pastry sheets, cut into quarters

MAKING: Crumble the Stilton evenly over the puff pastry and cook as per instructions on the pastry packet, then set aside. Make a poaching syrup in a pan with the water, sugar, wine, cinnamon and juice and zest of lemon. Add the pears and slowly poach, heating the liquid gently without boiling, until tender. Remove the pears from the liquid and reduce the poaching syrup by half.

FINISHING AND SERVING: Place one pear onto a serving dish, pour a little of the reduced liquid around and place one of the pastry squares alongside. Garnish with a dusting of icing sugar and serve.

Pumpkin Pie

This is quick to prepare, but is a very tasty dessert.

425g/15oz pumpkin puree
225g/8oz shortcrust pastry case
3 eggs
100g/4oz sugar, brown or white
½ tsp allspice
½ tsp cinnamon
¼ tsp nutmeg
¼ tsp salt
275ml/½ pt milk
Whipped cream to garnish

Preheat the oven to 200°C/400°F/Gas 6.

MAKING: Beat the eggs and mix in the spices, sugar and salt. Beat in the pumpkin puree, add the milk and then whisk. Pour the mix into the shortcrust pastry case, place the case directly onto the oven rack and bake for 40 minutes or until set.

FINISHING AND SERVING: Remove from the oven and serve warm with whipped cream. You can serve it hot or cold and use crème fraiche in place of the cream if preferred.

Raspberry Yoghurt Pie

Cook's Tip: Use different types of soft fruit for this dessert when in season.

400g/14oz fresh raspberries
175g/6oz wholemeal biscuit crumbs
100g/4oz butter
3tbsp icing sugar
2 egg whites
500ml/16fl oz plain thick yoghurt
200ml/7fl oz whipping cream
1tbsp powdered gelatine
1 lemon, juiced
Pinch salt
Whipped cream to decorate

MAKING: Melt the butter in a pan and add the biscuit crumbs. Mix well and transfer to a 23cm/9in pie dish, making sure to press out the crumb mix to cover the base of the dish. In a bowl, soften the gelatine with the lemon juice. Place the yoghurt in a different bowl and slowly add the dissolved gelatine, stirring well. In an additional two bowls, whip the cream and icing sugar together in one, and then beat the egg whites with the salt until stiff peaks form in the other. Add the whisked egg white and the cream and icing sugar mix to the yoghurt and pour in the raspberries. Mix well. Pour over the biscuit crust and chill.

FINISHING AND SERVING: When set, decorate with a little extra whipped cream and serve. Garnish the top with extra fruit pieces.

ERS

Strawberries in Cairn O'Mohr Strawberry Wine

FROM CAIRN O'MOHR WINERY
BY EDITH MOWATT

Cook's Tips: Make a sauce from the wine, by heating and reducing to a thick consistency, to pour over the fruit. Use a little dash of orange liqueur to enhance the strawberry flavour, and a few curls of orange zest as garnish to enhance the presentation. Chocolate-dipped strawberries would also be very effective. Use the smallest berries with the stalk remaining if possible, and dip them into melted chocolate. Adding butter to the chocolate produces a glossy finish.

1 punnet fresh strawberries
1 bottle Cairn O'Mohr Strawberry Wine

MAKING: Wash the strawberries and cut them into bite-sized pieces, then place them in a large bowl and cover with Cairn O'Mohr Strawberry Wine. Cover and leave to soak for two hours in the fridge.

SERVING: Serve with fresh, plain ice cream and brandy snaps. For an indulgent topping, add some shavings of dark chocolate or chocolate curls to the ice cream.

Strawberry Wine Velvet

FROM CAIRN O'MOHR WINERY
BY EDITH MOWATT

Cook's Tips: Try with some ratafia biscuits to provide a crunch. You could also add these to the bottom of the serving glass before pouring in the velvet.

300ml/½ pt whipping cream
200ml/⅓ pt Cairn O'Mohr Strawberry Wine
45g/2oz caster sugar
15ml/1tbsp clear honey
5 egg yolks
4 egg whites

MAKING: Mix the wine, honey and caster sugar together in a pan and add the egg yolks. Cook over a low heat, stirring constantly. As soon as the mixture thickens, plunge the pan into a basin of cold water to stop any further setting. Take care not to let any water into the mixture. Whisk the egg whites to soft peaks and whip the cream until stiff. Fold the whipped cream into the cooled mixture and, very gradually, spoon by spoon, add the whisked egg whites.

FINISHING AND SERVING: Mix well and pour into individual glasses, refrigerating until required. Serve garnished with a few chopped nuts and strawberries, or make a purée of strawberries and mint to decorate the velvet. To do so, crush the fresh strawberries through a sieve and season with chopped fresh mint leaves. A few chocolate curls on top of the velvet would also be effective.

Warm Berries in Liqueur and Citrus Cream

Cook's Tips: Frost the mint leaves by dipping them into egg white and then icing sugar. Add a few chocolate shavings into the bowl before the cream, or try soaking the berries in a chocolate liqueur instead of the Highland Liqueur.

250g/9oz seasonal berries such as strawberries, tayberries, redcurrants,
   or blackcurrants, washed and hulled
50ml/3fl oz Hebridean Liqueur
150ml/¼ pt double cream
1 orange, juice and zest
1 lime, juice and zest
Mint leaves as a garnish

MAKING: Put the berries into a bowl with the Hebridean Liqueur and allow to soak for 20 minutes. Put the cream into a mixing bowl, add the zest and juice of the orange and lime and mix well.

FINISHING AND SERVING: Put some of the berry mix into a suitable individual serving bowl, spoon over the citrus cream and serve cold with a couple of mint leaves as a garnish on top. Accompany with some Amaretto biscuits or brandy snaps. Use a frosted tall glass (place glass in freezer for 15 minutes) to serve and top with some roasted coconut or almonds for texture.

Chilli Sherry

FROM TOMBUIE SMOKEHOUSE
BY SALLY CRYSTAL

Cook's Tips: Use a low quality, very cheap sherry for this recipe, but don't use chillies that have blemishes on the skin.

1 bottle dry sherry
Quantity of fresh green and red chillies

MAKING: Wash and dry the chillies. Pour the sherry into a decanter and add sufficient chillies for about half the volume of the liquid. Leave to stand for six weeks, shaking the decanter occasionally.

SERVING: To use, add a few drops to soups, stews and casseroles, or add a kick to cream soups. Use sparingly as it is very potent!

Coleslaw

Cook's Tips: Cut the vegetables to an even size for best effect. Add a few pieces of citrus fruit – orange, lime or grapefruit – for variation. Mix in some nuts, such as crushed hazelnuts or chopped walnuts, or use a garlic or mustard-flavoured mayonnaise.

1 small white cabbage, cut into wedges and finely shredded
2 medium carrots, washed and grated
2 sticks celery, chopped
1 small finely-chopped onion
150ml/¼ pt mayonnaise

MAKING: Combine the carrot, cabbage, onion and celery in a bowl and mix well. Add the mayonnaise to the mixture and evenly coat the vegetables. Allow to stand for two hours before using.

Note: Without the dressing of the mayonnaise, this coleslaw will keep well in a sealed container in the fridge for a few days.

Crispy Croutons

FROM KNOWES FARM

Cook's Tips: To add a flavour to the croutons, preheat the oven to 175°C/350°F/Gas 4 and warm a greased baking sheet. Take the drained croutons, place on the warm baking sheet and sprinkle over some herbs, such as rosemary, basil or parsley. Return to the oven and bake for five minutes. Remove, allow to cool and serve. Try adding a little ground cheese or mustard powder as well.

1 cm/½ in thick slices of day old bread
Oil for frying

MAKING: Cut the crusts off the slices of bread and then cut the bread into evenly-sized cubes. Heat some oil in a frying pan, deep enough to just cover a cube of the bread. Add a single layer of bread cubes to the pan and fry, tossing occasionally, until the bread starts to colour.

FINISHING AND SERVING: Remove with a slotted spoon, drain well and allow to cool. Use as a garnish in soups and on salads.

Horseradish Sauce

Cook's Tip: Be careful when handling horseradish – it is just as potent as a hot chilli when fresh!

1 stick fresh horseradish, grated
100g/4oz white breadcrumbs
¼ tsp mustard
150ml/¼ pt milk
150ml/¼ pt whipped cream
1tbsp white wine vinegar

MAKING: Mix the grated horseradish with the mustard. Leave to marinade for one hour. Soak the breadcrumbs in the milk, leave to stand for 30 minutes and squeeze out the milk. Fold the drained breadcrumbs into the horseradish and mustard marinade, then add the white wine vinegar and whipped cream.

FINISHING AND SERVING: Season with a little salt and pepper and serve. (For a lighter sauce, use fromage frais.) This relish is excellent with smoked trout, simply served on fresh bread. You can also use it as a side dish with Trout and Almonds or other fish dishes, or with roast beef, served alongside boiled potatoes and vegetables.

Mulled Bouvrage

FROM ELLA DRINKS LTD

Bouvrage is a delicious soft drink made from the juice of real raspberries with a special flavour all its own. Made this way, it's a real winter warmer!

Cook's Tip: For a more 'adult' version, try adding a little brandy to the finished mulled Bouvrage.

750ml Bouvrage
2tbsp dark brown sugar
10cm stick cinnamon
$\frac{1}{2}$ tsp whole cloves
$\frac{1}{2}$ tsp sliced fresh ginger
3 or 4 slices each orange and lemon

MAKING: Pour the Bouvrage into a pan and add the sugar. Then add the cinnamon, broken into small pieces, cloves, ginger and the orange and lemon slices. Cover and gently heat until there is steam rising from the pan. Do not boil. Turn off the heat and allow to stand overnight to infuse the flavours. Strain and discard the spices and fruit. Return the Bouvrage infusion to the pan and heat very gently.

SERVING: Cover the pan between servings to retain the essence.

Olive Oil or Sunflower Oil Flavours

FROM TOMBUIE SMOKEHOUSE
BY SALLY CRYSTAL

Using an empty screw-top bottle and a good quality oil, depending on what flavour you desire, add:

Lemon rind or lemongrass stalks for a citrus flavour
Chillies (fresh or dried)
Peppercorns for a spicy flavour, garlic cloves, rosemary or other fresh herbs

PREPARING: Make sure that the bottles to be used are clean. Sterilise by filling with boiling water, draining and drying thoroughly in a low oven heat for 45 minutes.

MAKING: Pour the olive or sunflower oil into the clean bottles, and add the desired quantity of flavouring. Shake the jar, leave to settle and store before use.

Piccalilli

This is a classic accompaniment to cold game dishes, but will also go well with a number of recipes including fish and poultry.

Cook's Tips: Do not overcook the vegetables as they should be crunchy. You could pass the mixture through a sieve if you want a smooth sauce, but the vegetable pieces add a texture to the piccalilli that goes well with many dishes.

450g/1lb pickling onions
1 small cucumber
1 small cauliflower
225g/8oz tomatoes
225g/8oz French beans
100g/4oz cooking salt
100g/4oz granulated sugar
50g/2oz plain flour
50g/2oz mustard powder
25g/1oz turmeric
1.2L/2pt malt vinegar

MAKING: Chop all the vegetables into fine, equally-sized pieces, leaving the onions whole if very small. Place them in a bowl, sprinkle with the salt and mix well. Leave for 24 hours and drain. Mix the flour, sugar, mustard powder and turmeric and place in a pan. Blend to a paste with a little of the vinegar, then gradually add the rest of the vinegar over a low heat. Bring to the boil, stirring constantly until thick. Add the drained vegetables and simmer for three to five minutes.

STORING: Pour into hot, sterilised glass jars and seal, label and date.

Rhubarb and Fig Jam

FROM KNOWES FARM

Yield: about 5½ L/9pt

2kg/4lb rhubarb, washed and chopped into small pieces
2kg/4lb white sugar
5 lemons, juiced
500g/1lb dried figs, chopped and with stones and hard 'end bits' removed
Sterilised 1-gallon/½ l jars to store

MAKING: Place the rhubarb and sugar in a large glass or plastic bowl, sprinkle over the lemon juice and stir well. Place the figs in a separate bowl and cover with boiling water. Leave both bowls to stand overnight. When ready, tip all of the ingredients into a heavy-bottomed jam pan and boil for one hour or until thick. As the mixture froths during cooking, skim the residue off the surface.

FINISHING AND STORING: Pour the jam into hot, sterilised glass jars and seal immediately. Label and date the jam and store in a cool, dark and dry place. This jam will thicken considerably after cooling.

SERVING: Serve this as a spread on warm crusty white bread or stirred into hot rice pudding. As an alternative, warm slightly and use as an accompaniment to game dishes – spread it over duck breast in place of honey to glaze; or try on a roast ham in place of marmalade.

Rhubarb Sauce

FROM KNOWES FARM

Yield: about 6 servings

350g/12oz rhubarb stems, chopped
100g/4oz soft brown sugar
1/4 tsp allspice
250ml/8fl oz water

MAKING: Place all the ingredients in a pan, mix well and slowly bring to the boil. Stir well to dissolve the sugar. Simmer for ten minutes, stirring occasionally. Remove from heat and pass through a sieve.

SERVING: Serve either hot or cold. This sauce goes well with ice cream, pies or even on sponge cakes.

Spicy Tomato Chutney

Cook's Tips: For the best flavour, warm the chutney slightly in a pan, as this will bring out the flavours better than if served cold. To easily remove the skin of the tomato, put a cross in the side of the tomato, push onto the end of a skewer and hold in a gas flame. As the heat blackens the skin it will easily peel away. Another method is to put a slit in the side of the tomato, place in a jug of boiling water for 30 seconds, then easily slip off the skin and discard.

450g/1lb tomatoes, washed and skin removed
225g/8oz Demerara sugar
2 chillies, chopped
2 cloves garlic, crushed
2.5cm/1in piece ginger root, grated
1tbsp balsamic vinegar
1tbsp red wine vinegar
1tbsp fish sauce

MAKING: Divide the tomatoes into two batches, puree half of them and place in a pan. Roughly chop the remaining tomatoes and place in the same pan. Add the remaining ingredients, bring to the boil and reduce to a simmer for 40 minutes.

FINISHING AND STORING: Pour into hot, sterilised jars, label and date. Store in a cool, dark place. The chutney will keep for up to one month.

SERVING: Serve with plain grilled fish or cold meats, or use as a glaze on chicken or hams when roasting. Also try serving in a little washed lettuce leaf 'basket' as a side dish. For this, simply wash a small crispy lettuce leaf, put the chutney on the inside of the leaf and place it with the rib of the leaf facing down.

Sublime Mayonnaise

FROM KINTALINE PLANT AND POULTRY CENTRE

Cook's Tip: By making this a few times, you will become familiar with the exact amount of oil required to achieve the best consistency of the mayonnaise.

2 large eggs
Sunflower oil as required
1tsp dry English mustard powder
1tbsp white wine vinegar
Salt and pepper to season

MAKING: Break whole eggs into the bowl on a blender or liquidiser. Add the English mustard powder and a good seasoning of salt and pepper. Turn on the blender to a medium speed and mix the above for 45 seconds. Reduce the speed to the lowest setting and very slowly pour in a thin trickle of sunflower oil until there is about 6cm/2½ in of mix in the bowl. *Note: The exact quantity of oil will depend on the size of eggs used.* Keep blending at a low speed until the mix becomes firm. If it is almost set you have enough oil, though more can be added if needed.

FINISHING AND SERVING: Once ready, transfer to a bowl and add the white wine vinegar, stirring well. Chill in the refrigerator before serving. Divide the mayonnaise into small bowls and try adding a few different flavours, such as: tarragon, garlic and parsley for serving with chicken; lemon juice and dill for salmon; or tomato puree and redcurrant jelly for lamb.

Brandy Snaps

120g/4oz sieved flour
240g/9oz golden syrup
140g/5oz caster sugar
90g/3oz butter
6g/¼oz of ground ginger

Preheat the oven to 215°C/425°F/Gas 7.

MAKING: Cream together the caster sugar and butter. Add the flour and fold in the ginger and golden syrup. When mixed to a smooth paste, put into a piping bag with a narrow, plain nozzle. Pipe into 1cm/¼in rounds on a greased baking tray, allowing space for the mixture to spread while cooking. Bake for five minutes or until the edges are just brown and the whole surface is golden. Allow to cool slightly until just firm and roll round the handle of a wooden spoon which will create the round tube of the brandy snap.

FINISHING AND SERVING: Slip off the handle and allow to cool before serving. Serve with a filling of whipped cream, flavoured with a liqueur, or with desserts such as cranachan or apple water ice.

Butter Biscuits

Yield: 25-30 biscuits

225g/8oz flour
175g/6oz caster sugar
125g/4oz butter
1 egg
5ml/1tsp cream of tartar
2.5ml/½ tsp bicarbonate of soda
Few drops vanilla extract

Preheat the oven to 175°C/350°F/Gas 4.

MAKING: Cream the butter with the sugar until light, add the egg and vanilla and beat. Into the same bowl, sift the flour, add the cream of tartar and bicarbonate of soda and mix well. Turn out and knead until a smooth dough is formed. Form into small balls about the size of a walnut, flatten lightly using a fork to make the shape of the biscuit and bake for 12-15 minutes.

FINISHING AND SERVING: Cool on a wire rack and serve. Place a slice of date or glace cherry on each biscuit for decoration.

Cheese Pastry

Cook's Tips: To make twists, simply give the straws a couple of turns before baking. Add sesame seeds to the mix for a different taste.

125g/4oz plain flour
60g/2oz butter
60g/2oz cheddar cheese, finely grated
1 egg yolk
1tbsp water
Pinch cayenne pepper
Pinch salt

Preheat the oven to 175°C/350°F/Gas 4.

MAKING: Sieve the flour, salt and cayenne together in a bowl and rub in the butter until the mixture resembles fine breadcrumbs. Add the finely-grated cheese, the egg yolk and the water. Mix well into a firm dough. Roll out onto a floured board and cut into straws or discs.

FINISHING AND SERVING: Bake for ten minutes until crisp. Serve them as a biscuit or crumble into soup. Decorate the top of the discs with a little cream cheese, crushed nuts or extra-grated cheese. Serve with various cream cheese dips such as roast onion, sweet red pepper, garlic or blue cheese. For this, simply add the flavour to good quality cream cheese or mayonnaise and serve with a garnish of parsley.

Cheese Scones

250g/8oz self-raising flour
125g/4oz cheddar cheese, grated
60g/2oz butter
¼ tsp salt
Milk to mix
1 egg, beaten

Preheat the oven to 200°C/400°F/Gas 6.

MAKING: Sift together the flour and salt, rub in the butter and add the grated cheese. Gradually add enough milk to make a soft dough. Turn onto a floured board and knead lightly for a few minutes. Roll out to about 2cm/³⁄₄ in thick. Cut into rounds, put on a baking sheet and brush with beaten egg.

FINISHING AND SERVING: Bake at the top of the oven for seven to ten minutes, remove and allow to cool before serving.

Fat Rascals

FROM HEATHERSLAW CORN MILL

250g/9oz self-raising flour
125g/4oz lard
85g/3oz sugar
60g/2oz currants
30g/1oz sultanas
Pinch salt
Water or beaten egg

Preheat the oven to 215°C/425°F/Gas 7.

MAKING: Rub the lard into the flour and then add all the other ingredients, mixing into a soft dough with a little water or beaten egg. Roll out into a sheet approximately ½ in deep and cut into rounds. Bake for about 15 minutes or until browned.

SERVING: Cool on a wire rack before serving.

Cinnamon Jam Bake

300g/11oz plain flour
250g/9oz soft butter
200g/7oz sugar
175g/6oz smooth apricot jam
125g/4oz grated coconut
1 egg
5ml/1tsp vanilla essence
5ml/1tsp cinnamon
5ml/1tsp baking powder
Pinch salt

Preheat the oven to 175°C/350°F/Gas 4.

MAKING: Cream the butter and sugar together in a large bowl. Beat the egg with the vanilla and add to the butter and sugar. Mix the plain flour, baking powder, salt and cinnamon and add to the same bowl. Mix again so all the ingredients are bound together and work into a soft dough. Place ²⁄₃ of the dough into a greased baking tin (30cmx20cm/13inx8in) and spread the jam over the surface. With the remaining dough, mix in the coconut and grate this over the top of the jam. Dust with a little extra cinnamon if desired, and bake for 20-25 minutes.

SERVING: In the baking tin, cut into bars, allow to cool and move onto a wire rack until cold.

Easy Oat Slice

Cook's Tips: Add a few chopped dates, cherries or raisins to add a fruit flavour to the slices. Try it with sunflower seeds for a nutty alternative. You can leave out the coconut if preferred.

175g/6oz porridge oats
150g/5oz sugar
125g/4oz white or brown flour
90g/3oz desiccated coconut
150g/5oz butter
30ml/2tbsp golden syrup
5ml/1tsp bicarbonate of soda

Preheat the oven to 175°C/350°F/Gas 4.

MAKING: Mix the oats, sugar, flour and coconut together in a large bowl. In a separate bowl, melt the butter, add the golden syrup and bicarbonate of soda and, when it foams, stir into the oat mix. Mix well and pour into a greased baking tray. Bake for 15 minutes.

FINISHING AND SERVING: Cut into squares and remove from the tin when cold.

Heatherslaw's Carrot Cake

FROM HEATHERSLAW CORN MILL

Cook's Tips: For an easy cream cheese topping, mix together 500g/18oz sifted icing sugar, 45g/1½oz soft butter and 90g/3oz cream cheese and spread over the top of the carrot cake. Add a few drops of vanilla essence if preferred. For an alternative flavour, add 1tsp of either grated lemon, orange or lime rind and a little of the same fruit juice. Garnish the topping with walnut halves or thin slices of carrot, blanched so that they wilt.

Note: The margarine can be substituted with butter.

175g/6oz Heatherslaw's wholemeal flour
120g/4oz grated carrot
120g/4oz margarine
120g/4oz soft brown sugar
2 large eggs
1tbsp milk
2½ level tsp baking powder
½ orange, grated zest
Pinch salt
1tsp cinnamon (optional)

Preheat the oven to 160°C/325°F/Gas 3.

MAKING: Grease a 15cm/6in cake tin, line it with greaseproof paper and set to one side. Sift the baking powder, salt, flour and cinnamon (if using) into a small bowl and mix well. Then add the grated carrot, mixing again. In a separate large bowl, cream together the margarine and sugar until light and 'fluffy', then add the orange zest. Add the eggs one at a time to the margarine and sugar mix, beating them in thoroughly. Spoon a little of the flour mix on top to prevent curdling. Gradually mix in the rest of the flour and add the milk a little at a time until the mixture is soft, but not runny. Pour into the prepared cake tin and cook for 45-60 minutes.

FINISHING AND SERVING: Turn out and cool on a wire rack before serving.

Heatherslaw's Lemon Cake

FROM HEATHERSLAW CORN MILL

Cook's Tip: A good thick dairy ice cream would also work well when serving this cake.

Note: The margarine can be substituted with butter.

175g/6oz Heatherslaw's wholemeal flour
1tsp baking powder
3 eggs
175g/6oz soft margarine
175g/6oz soft brown sugar
1 thin-skinned lemon, thinly sliced
Pinch mixed spice

Preheat the oven to 160°C/325°F/Gas 3.

MAKING: Grease a 20cm/8in cake tin and line it with greaseproof paper. Cover the base of the tin with the thin slices of lemon. Cream together all the rest of the ingredients and pour into the cake tin. Cook for 30-40 minutes until the surface is golden brown.

FINISHING AND SERVING: Remove from the oven and leave in the tin for a further ten minutes before turning out and serving 'upside down' with the lemon slices on the top. Serve this with a creamy, cool crème fraiche or try with sour cream. If you haven't any in the house, simply take some single cream, stir in a teaspoon of lemon juice and let stand at room temperature for 30 minutes before using. Garnish the top with a curl or two of lemon zest and drizzle over some warmed lemon liqueur.

Hot Cross Buns

FROM HEATHERSLAW CORN MILL

Yield: approximately 20 buns

225g/8oz Heatherslaw's wholemeal flour
225g/8oz strong white flour
30g/1oz fresh OR 15g/½oz dried yeast
120g/4oz currants
60g/2oz soft brown sugar
60g/2oz butter
2tsp mixed spice
2 eggs
150ml/¼pt milk
1 level tsp salt

Preheat the oven to 200°C/400°F/Gas 6.

MAKING: Warm the milk and use a small amount to cream the yeast, then set
to one side. In a large bowl, mix both of the flours with the salt, sugar and mixed
spices. Make a well in the centre and add the creamed yeast. Add the butter, eggs
and sufficient milk to make a soft but firm dough. Add the currants, and knead
the dough thoroughly to distribute them evenly. Cover and leave in a warm place
to rise for about two hours or until it has doubled in size. Knead the dough again
briefly and either fill greased bun tins to ⅔ full or form the dough into bun
shapes and place on a greased oven tray allowing space for a second rising.
Smooth the tops of the buns into a dome shape and leave in a warm place to
double in size again. If available, press strips of pastry to form a cross on the top
of each bun, or just score the top with a knife to make a cross in the dough. Bake
for 15-20 minutes until cooked.

FINISHING AND SERVING: Remove the buns from the oven and, while still
hot, glaze the tops with a little sugar dissolved in warm water. Store in an airtight
container and warm slightly before serving.

Mrs J Cowen's Prize-winning Bamburgh Biscuits

FROM HEATHERSLAW CORN MILL

These biscuits won first prize at the Bamburgh WI and those girls know their biscuits!

175g/6oz Heatherslaw wholemeal flour
45g/1½oz Heatherslaw oat bran
75g/3oz unsalted butter
50g/2oz raw brown sugar
3tbsp milk
5ml/1tsp baking powder
½tsp salt
Brown sugar crystals to decorate

Preheat the oven to 175°C/350°F/Gas 4.

MAKING: Mix all the dry ingredients except the sugar together. Rub in the butter until the mixture resembles fine breadcrumbs. Stir in the sugar and add the milk. Stir well until the dough is firm but manageable. Roll out thinly onto a floured board and stamp out rounds from the dough. Place on a greased baking sheet and press brown sugar crystals onto the top of each biscuit. Bake for ten minutes.

FINISHING AND SERVING: Cool on a wire rack before serving. These biscuits will store well in an airtight container.

Oatmeal Bread

FROM HEATHERSLAW CORN MILL

340g/12oz Heatherslaw wholemeal flour
225g/8oz rolled oats
30g/1oz fresh or 15g/½oz 'fast action' yeast
1tsp honey
2 level tsp salt
1tbsp sunflower oil
300ml/½pt warm milk
150ml/¼pt warm water

Preheat the oven to 200°C/400°F/Gas 6.

MAKING: Pour the milk over the oats and leave for 30 minutes. Dissolve the honey in the warm water, add the yeast and set aside until frothy. Mix the flour and salt in a bowl, and add the oil, yeast mix and oat mixture. Mix well to a soft dough, turn onto a floured board and knead for ten minutes. Return the dough to an oiled bowl, cover and leave to stand in a warm place until doubled in size. This should take approximately one hour. Knead and knock back the dough for a further three minutes, then place it in either one greased 2lb tin or two greased 1lb tins. Leave to rise again for about 40 minutes. Bake on the middle or top shelf of the oven for 30-35 minutes.

FINISHING AND SERVING: Remove from the oven and, to test if done, tap the bottom of the cooked loaf. If it does not sound hollow, return to the tin and cook for a further five to ten minutes. Allow to cool on a wire rack before serving.

Pat's Scones

FROM HEATHERSLAW CORN MILL

Cook's Tips: Substitute the sultanas with date or apricot pieces. Replace the sugar and fruit with 100g/4oz grated cheese, a pinch of herbs and a teaspoon of mustard powder for a savoury alternative.

Note: The margarine can be substituted with butter.

Yield: approximately 12 scones

225g/8oz Heatherslaw wholemeal flour
30g/1oz margarine
1 level tsp baking powder
45g/1½oz sugar
60g/2oz sultanas
150ml/¼pt milk
Pinch salt
Milk or egg for glazing

Preheat the oven to 175°C/350°F/Gas 4.

MAKING: In a large bowl, mix together the flour, salt and baking powder. Rub in the margarine and add the sugar and fruit. Bind the mixture with the milk and knead until smooth. Do not roll, but press the dough out lightly to about 1cm thick, and separate into about 12 scones. Place them on a greased baking tray and glaze with a milk or egg wash. Allow to rest for five minutes, then bake for 15-20 minutes.

SERVING: Cool before serving. Hot scones are often served as a breakfast dish in the USA, but are called biscuits. Try the savoury version warm with extra butter.

Shortbread

250g/9oz plain flour
175g/6oz icing sugar
175g/6oz butter
2tbsp cornflour
Pinch salt

Preheat the oven to 150°C/300°F/Gas 2.

MAKING: Sift the flour, cornflour, icing sugar and salt together in a bowl and mix together. Rub in the butter until crumbly. Knead well and roll out to about 2cm/³⁄₄in thickness onto the base of a loose-bottomed, ungreased 23cm/9in cake tin. With a fork, make a pattern around the edge of the shortcake to decorate and prick all over the surface. Bake for 45 minutes.

FINISHING AND SERVING: Remove from the oven and allow to stand in the tin for five minutes before slicing. Once sliced, allow to cool completely on a rack.

Sugar Free Banana Bar

BY HENDERSONS BAKERY

Cook's Tip: This recipe is vegan, wheat free and has no added sugar, as the sweetness comes from the natural sugars in the bananas.

400g/14oz peeled bananas
180ml/⅓ pt sunflower oil
140g/5oz cashew nuts
140g/5oz oats
140g/5oz shredded coconut
140g/5oz raisins
15g/½ oz cinnamon
15g/½ oz nutmeg

Preheat the oven to 175°C/350°F/Gas 4.

MAKING: Mix the bananas and sunflower oil until smooth and creamy. Add all the other ingredients, mixing lightly until bound together. Press into a greased flan dish. Bake in the middle of the oven for 15 minutes or until the surface is golden brown.

SERVING: Allow to cool and cut into small wedges. Try serving with sour cream and chocolate shavings for a really special treat!

DIRECTORY OF PRODUCERS

The following list details the producers and growers that attend the majority of the Farmers' Markets in Scotland. If you have access to the internet, up-to-date information about the operation of the Markets as a whole and a further list of the producers can be found at the website for the Scottish Association of Farmers' Markets at www.scottishfarmersmarkets.co.uk.

There is a short list at the end of this section with the addresses of a few useful websites with links to various Markets, suppliers and home shopping that may be of interest. There are a wide variety of goods available at the various Farmers' Markets in Scotland, with some operators finding that there is such a demand from producers that they have a waiting list for suppliers who wish to bring their goods to the Market.

This, in fact, allows the operators of the Markets, who are often farmers themselves, to be able to ensure that the produce available at any one time is of the highest quality. A few craft items are available at a number of the Markets, such as wood turning, hand-knitted clothing and beeswax candles. General goods and house-wares etc, are specifically excluded from Farmers' Markets though as there are strict criteria for the type of goods that can be offered.

Please bear in mind that the information below is of course subject to change and if you are seeking a particular ingredient or item, please visit your local Market in the first instance to check the stock of the local producer.

The list is arranged by type of produce with business name, contact name and telephone number. Every effort has been made to ensure that the details are correct but should you experience any difficulties in contacting any of the producers, please contact the Scottish Association of Farmers' Markets.

BEEF

Aberdeen Angus Direct	Erskine	Matthew Stevenson	0141 8120220
Allershaw Farm Meat	Biggar	Alastair McArthur	01864 505234
Bannerman Quality Meat	Drymen	Gilbert Bannerman	01360 870210
Barkers Highland Beef	Callander	Hilary Barker	01877 330203
Wm Bell & Sons	Bridge of Earn	Mr Bell	01738 812580
Binn Farm	Glenfarg	Colin MacGregor	01577 830305
Blackmount Meats	Dunsyre	Alex Allison	01698 682250
Braes of Coul Beef & Lamb	Kirriemuir	George Patullo	01575 560714
Brig Highland Beef	Bridge of Earn	Joanne McKenzie	01738 812456
Candy Farm Produce	Abernethy	Hazel Robertson	01738 850432
Carmichael Estates Farm Meats	Biggar	Richard Carmichael	01899 308336
David McTear Butchers	Gorebridge	David McTear	01875 822968
Dornoch Farm Butchers	Dornoch	Darren or Alex	01862 810334
Garleton Prime Beef	North Berwick	John Sheddon	01620 880511
J & M Stewart	St Andrews	John Stewart	01334 473061
J W Kay & Co	Straiton	Shonaid Kay	01655 770217
Jamesfield Organic Farm	Abernethy	Ian Miller	01738 850498
John Young & Sons	New Cumnock	Walter Young	01290 338562
Kinloss Farms Ltd	Cupar	Chris Addison-Scott	01334 654169
Lurgan Farm Shop	Aberfeldy	Sally Murray	01887 829303
Mrs Hamilton's Beef & Lamb	Kirknewton	Caroline Hamilton	01506 881510
Orkney Viking Beef	Kirkwall	Tom Flett	01856 761371
Reiver Country Foods	Eyemouth	Adam Marshall	01890 761355
Speyside Organics	Aberlour	James Fraser	01340 810484

Guaranteed traceability. All meat sold comes from animals barn reared and finished in our farm. No forced feeding, fertilisers, chemicals, sprays, routine medications used. All beef hung for a minimum of 21 days. Order at Farmers' Markets, email, phone & mail order. Members: Scottish Association Farmers' Markets / SOPA 14831 / SFQC Approved Scheme Mark 13197. Email: jandcfraser@aol.com. Find us at the Farmers' Market at: Inverness / Aberdeen

Stewarton Farm	Peebles	Hazel Clarke	01721 730755
The Store	Ellon	Andrew Booth	01358 788083
Well Hung and Tender	Berwick On Tweed	Sarah McPherson	01289 286216

Home produced Aberdeen Angus beef direct from our prize-winning herd. Hung–on–the–bone for 21 days minimum (and up to 35 days). Pre-packed and cut to specification. Winners of Farmers Weekly 'Battle of the Beef' competition October 2003 at Eastbourne. Order at Farmers' Markets, internet, phone & mail order. Members: Farm Retail Association. Email: info@wellhungandtender.com Web: www.wellhungandtender.com. Find us at the Farmers' Market at: Edinburgh.

BAKING AND BAKERY PRODUCTS

Bush Cottage Products	Eyemouth	Mrs Blades	01890 761226
Cakes For Special People	Edinburgh	Sarah Thomson	0131 552 2079

Delicious home-made cakes that really taste as you would want them to had you made them yourself! Includes a selection of cakes that are sugar-free, plus gluten and wheat free. Probably the best cake stall in Scotland. Order at Farmers' Markets. Member: Scottish Association Farmers' Markets. Email: stsc19922@blueyonder.co.uk. Find us at the Farmers' Market at: Glasgow-Partick / Barrhead / Greenock / Kirkcaldy / Lomond Shores.

Caledonia Homebakes	Blairgowrie	Joanna Henderson	01250 884740
Campbells Bakery	Crieff	Iain Campbell	01764 780964
Country Bakes	Huntly	Muriel Duguid	01466 780964
Country Bytes	Bridge of Weir	Iona Young	01505 615803
Elfis Homebaking	Nairn	Elfi Whyte	01667 455023
Grannys Goodys	Inverness	Helen Nichilson	01463 831496
Heatherslaw Cornmill	Cornhill on Tweed	John Murphy	01890 820338

We provide stoneground wholemeal flour, plain white, rye flour and barley flour, wheatgerm, bran, pearl barley, barley kernels, de-luxe muesli, oatmeals and Scottish rolled oatflakes. Order at Farmers' Markets. Member: Scottish Association Farmers' Markets; National Association Farmers Markets. Email: tourism@ford-and-etal.co.uk Web: www.ford-and-etal.co.uk. Find us at the Farmers' Market at: Edinburgh / Peebles / Holy Island (Seasonal) plus more Farmers' Markets to come.

Hendersons	Edinburgh	Hazel Miller	0131 225 2131

Hand-crafted bread, organic oatcakes and loaf cakes, prepared using the finest ingredients including organic flour and made with no additives, preservatives or GM products. Order at Farmers' Markets. Member: Soil Association. Email: mail@hendersonsofedinburgh.co.uk. Web: www.hendersonsofedinburgh.co.uk. Find us at the Farmers' Market at: Edinburgh / Glasgow / Perth / Stirling.

JAK Celebration Cakes	Biggar	Jennifer Anne Kennedy	01899 221437
MacPhails Bakery	Cupar	Fiona MacPhail	01334 654147
Mary's Marvellous Munchables	Maybole	Mary Dunlop	01655 770231
Parduvine Pantry	Rosewell	Mary Logan	01875 830239
Paulines Pantry	Rogart	Pauline Child	01408 64287
Petrie Fine Foods	Dunlop	Howard Wilkinson	01560 484861
Eva Schulte	Cupar	Eva Schulte	07753 846447
The Oatmeal of Alford	Laurence kirk	John Medlock	01561 377356
Trusty Crust Organic Bakery	East Saltoun	Peter Hamilton	01875 340939
Valvona & Crolla	Edinburgh		0131 556 6066

CHEESE AND DAIRY PRODUCE

Allathan Dairy	Turiff	Pat Coutts	01771 644369
Caithness Cheese	Occumster	Sandra Sutherland	01593 721309
Doddington Dairy	Wooler	Jackie Maxwell	01668 283010
Dunlop Dairy Products	Stewarton	Ann Dorward	01560 482494
Hand Made Cheese Company	Dalry	Hazel Forsyth	01294 832479
Stichills Jerseys	Kelso	Brenda Leddy	01573 470263

CONFECTIONERY

Finishing Touches	Glasgow	Heather Green	0141 942 2226
Gordon & Durwood	Crieff		01764 653800
Hannahs Kitchen	Inverness	Richard Halifax	01463 243524
Jennie Betts	Ardgay	Jennie Betts	01862 893253
Knowehead Products	Newburgh	Alison Batchelor	01337 841090
Threepwood Fayre	Beith	John Dobbie	01505 503553

CRAFTS

Batty Little Women (Silks)	Inverness	Anne Youngman	01381 610480
Ken Bell Artwork (Art)	Munlochy	Ken Bell	01463 811762
Caurnie Soap Co (Soaps)	Kirkintilloch	Jim Little	0141 776 1218

We believe passionately that soap is best made by cold process double saponification. We provide gentle soaps with an addictive concoction of choices for every type of skin. Our organic Rosemary and Tea Tree shampoo can be filled into your own bottles environmentally! Order at Farmers' Markets, email, phone and mail order.
Email: office@caurnie.com Web: www.caurnie.com. Find us at the Farmers' Market at: Edinburgh / Glasgow-Partick / Lomond Shores / Kilsyth / Aberfeldy / Blairgowrie / Stirling / Dundee.

Coach House Products (Furniture)	Tain	Ian MacKenzie	01862 892325
Dalchards Love crafts (Cards, etc)	Tain	Helga Dharmpaul	01862 852460
Dark Fibres (Paper goods)	Lairg	Joanna Gair	01971 521245
Elizabeth McNicoll (Jewellery)	Tain	Elizabeth McNicoll	01862 894160
Hartmount Woodturning			
(Wood items)	Northallerton	Paul Turner	01609 777233
Highland Wildwoods (Flowers)	Fortrose	Trish McKeggie	01381 621040
Jewelcraft (Gifts)	Tain	Nichola MacDonald	01862 871848
Kate Sharp Knitwear			
(Handknitting)	Humbie	Kate Sharp	01875 833215
Reflections (Candles, crafts)	Inverness	Gwen Stewart	01463 221919
Rogart Craft Workshop			
(Candles, gifts)	Rogart	Mrs Laurence O'Neill	01408 641473
The Soap Box (Soaps)	Seahouses	Mrs Chris Jones	01665 720263

DRINKS

Black Isle Brewery	Munlochy	David Gladwin	01463 811871
Burnswell Spring Water	Mauchline	Andrew Cooper	01290 550705
Cairn O'Mohr Fruit Wines	Errol	Ron Gilles	01821 642781

We produce delicious leaf and berry wines fermented from fresh Scottish soft fruits, leaves, berries and flowers. Available in Strawberry, Raspberry, Bramble, Elderberry, Oak Leaf and Elderflower. All produced with unique Celtic designs, our wines look good and taste great! Order at Farmers' Markets, internet, phone & mail order. Member: Scottish Association Farmers' Markets. Email: us@cairnomohr.co.uk Web: www.cairnomohr.co.uk. Find us at the Farmers' Market at: Edinburgh / Glasgow / Paisley / Falkirk / Clarkston / Blairgowrie.

Ella Drinks Ltd	Alloa	Anne Thomson	01786 834342

Bouvrage Raspberry drink. Enjoy the biting freshness and wonderful aroma of Scotland's famous raspberries in an all-natural real juice drink. The wonderful aroma and flavour produce a superb clean, crisp drink, either on its own or to accompany any meal! Order at Farmers' Markets Member: Scottish Association Farmers' Markets. Email info@bouvrage.com. Web: www.bouvrage.com. Find us at the Farmers' Market at: Edinburgh / Glasgow / Paisley / Falkirk / Clarkston / Aberdeen / Inverurie / Dundee / Cupar / Stirling / Lomond Shores / Perth / Ayr / Rutherglen / Angus.

Houston Brewing Company	Houston	Carl Wengel	07768 472996
Hebridean Liqueur Company	Helensburgh	Roy Lewis	01436 679935
Scots Cheer	East Linton	Derry Campbell	01620 860914
Scottish Mead Company	West Kilbride	Lynne Wallace	01294 823222
Scottish Liqueur Centre	Perth		01738 787044

FRUITS AND VEGETABLES

A P Barrie & Co	Couper Angus		01828 628660
Bellfield Organic Nursery	Strathmiglo	Derek Alexander	01337 860764
The Crisp Hut	Edinburgh	Nick Paul	07855 814668

Hand made, real potato crisps. Farm fresh potatoes, cooked on demand and seasoned with a range of tempting flavours. For the finest and freshest crisps, ready to eat or ideal for taking home and enjoying hot later on – they really do reheat extremely well – look for our bespoke mobile units at events and Markets throughout the year. Order at Farmers' Markets. Email: mail@crisphut.com Web: www.crisphut.com. Find us at the Farmers' Markets at: Edinburgh / Paisley / Glasgow / Airdrie / Greenock / Cupar / Kirkcaldy / St Andrews (occasional market) / Lomond Shores, plus various events, game shows and fairs.

C S Chalmers & Son	Dundee	Colin Chalmers	01382 360394
J Chalmers	Blairgowrie	Jim Chalmers	01738 583839
Clayfolds Farm	Banff	George Addison	01261 821288

FRUITS AND VEGETABLES CONTINUED...

J & M Craig	Carluke	Jim Craig	01555 860279
Dalchonzie Farm Shop	Comrie	Barbara Burberry	01764 670416
Dounepark Farms	Banff	Duncan Dickson	01261 812121
East Coast Organic	Tranemt	Mike Callender	01875 340227
John Hannah Tomato Growers Ltd	Cleghorn	John Hannah	01555 663002
Hendersons	Edinburgh	Hazel Miller	0131 225 2131
Keyden Cottage	Brechin	A Watson	01356 622953
Knowes Farm	Dunbar	Hilary Cochran	01620 860010

Knowes Farm Shop provides a unique range of home-grown, home-made local and Scottish fresh produce and foods. We grow 'Sun & Dung' naturally fertilised, spray-free vegetables plus free-range eggs. We make preserves, soups, pates and pavlovas. Order at Farmers' Markets. Member: Farm Retail Association; Scottish Egg Producer Retailer Association; FWAG; Natures Choice. Email. peter@knowes.demon.co.uk. Web: www.knowes.com. Find us at the Farmers' Markets at: Edinburgh / Haddington.

Lanchester Fruit	Lanchester	Johnathon Benson	01207 528805

We produce single variety apple juice, mainly using apples that are not usually available. Apple and Elderflower, Apple and Rhubarb, Apple and Redcurrant and Apple and Strawberry juice are also made. Available in 20cl and 70cl bottles through retail. Order at Farmers' Markets. Find us at the Farmers' Markets at: Edinburgh / Haddington / Alnwick / Morpeth / Newcastle / Barnard Castle / Orton / Murton / Ryedale / Darlington plus major shows.

Laprig Farm Vegetables	Greenlaw	John Fleming	01890 840215
David Leslie Fruits	Perth	David Leslie	01738 551135
W H Macfadzean & Sons	Kilmarnock	Robin MacFadzean	01563 884272
Milton Haugh Farm Shop	Arbroath	Lesley Gray	01241 875364

Available at Milton Haugh are: corn-fed, free-range chickens; free-range eggs; vegetables and potatoes; tasty ready-made meals; jellies, jams, marmalades and honeys, all produced by us on the Farm. The adjoining Corn Kist Coffee House serves delicious baking and soups, etc, all made in our own kitchens. Order at Farmers' Markets. Member: Farm Retail Association; Scottish Association Farmers' Markets.
Email: info@miltonhaugh.com Web: www.miltonhaugh.com. Find us at the Farmers' Markets at: Forfar, plus Dundee Food and Flower Show.

Overton Farm Shop	Carluke	John Young	01555 860226
George Pinkerton Ltd	Johnstone	Iain Pinkerton	01505 612250
David Randall & Son	Blairgowrie	David Randall	01250 872237
The Really Garlicky Co	Nairn	Gilli Allingham	01667 45219
Skye & Lochalsh Horticultural Developers Assoc	Carbost	Catrina MacDonald	01478 640276
Thisselcockrig Fruit & Vegetables	Duns	Jock Bolton	01890 870370

FRUITS AND VEGETABLES CONTINUED...

Carroll's Heritage Potatoes	Coldstream	Anthony and Lucy Carroll	01890 883 795

The Carroll's farm is at Tiptoe Northumberland, in the spectacularly beautiful River Till valley. They specialise in growing ten heritage varieties of potatoes, which are gourmet, offering delicious flavours, interesting colours, shapes and flexibility for culinary uses with a unique taste of history. Order at Farmers' Markets, email and phone. Member: National Association Farmers Markets; Farm Retail Association; LEAF.
Email: info@heritage-potatoes.co.uk Web: www.heritage-potatoes.co.uk. Find us at the Farmers' Markets at: Edinburgh / Glasgow.

Valvona & Crolla	Edinburgh		0131 556 6066
Wester Hardmuir Fruit Farm	Nairn	James Clark	01309 641259

FISH AND SEAFOOD

Belhaven Trout Company	Dunbar	David Pate	01368 863244
Caledonian Oysters	Oban	Judith Vajk	01631 710397
Castlegate	Banff	Billy Gatt	01261 812239
Creelers Seafood Restaurants	Edinburgh	Tim James	0131 220 4447
Drummond Trout Farm and Fishery	Comrie	Simon Barnes	01764 670500

Delicious fresh and smoked trout noted for their exceptional flavour. Drummond Trout have an enviable reputation. You can catch Drummond Trout at the Farm, one of the top attractions in Perthshire, or buy direct from many Farmers' Markets. Order at Farmers' Markets, email, phone or mail order. Member: Scottish Association Farmers' Markets; National Association Farmers Markets. Email: simon@drummondtroutfarm.co.uk Web: wwwdrummondtroutfarm.co.uk. Find us at the Farmers' Markets at: Edinburgh / Perth / Glasgow / Stirling / Cupar / Kirkcaldy / Dundee/ St Andrews (occasional market).

Dunkeld Smoked Salmon	Dunkeld	Angela Scott	01350 727369
Fencebay Fisheries	Fairlie	Jill Thain	01475 568918
MacMillan Foods	Campbeltown	Archie MacMillan	01586 553580
Halliday & Lloyd Ltd	Montrose	Mike Lloyd	07979 595601
Marinades of Scotland	Kelty	Catriona Cairney	01383 839598
Ocean Bleu Ltd	West Kilbride	Rankin Durnin	01294 822444
Peatland Smokehouse	Gatehead	Hywel Davies	01563 850850
Iain R Spink	Alness	Iain Spink	01349 884169

Arbroath Smokies and trout, smoked in the traditional way over an open hardwood fire in a half whisky barrel. Produce can be kept refrigerated for six to seven days, or freezes well. We even take the bones out for you! Order at Farmers' Markets.
Email: iainandsu@tesco.net. Find us at the Farmers' Markets at: Cupar plus at many Highland Games and Game fairs during the summer. More Farmers' Market planned!

Tarradale Game Ltd	Muir of Ord	Robert Urquhart	01463 871145
Tombuie Smokehouse	Aberfeldy	David Crystal	01887 820127

GAME AND VENISON

C & R White	Kinross	Roy White	01577 840310
Donora Farms	Forfar	Heather Gow	01307 462437
Fair and Square Game Butchery	Crianlarich	David Nicolson	01567 820975
Fletchers of Auchtermuchty	Auchtermuchty	Nicola Fletcher	01337 828369
Heritage Meat and Game	Kilbarchan	Sean Middleton	01505 612451
Hilton Wild Boar	Perth	Andrew Johnston	01337 842867
Tombuie Smokehouse	Aberfeldy	David Crystal	01887 820127

This award-winning smokehouse was established in 1991 as part of the farm's diversification and is known for the quality of its smoked meats, cheeses, fresh venison and lamb. Visit the Tombuie Smokehouse custom-built sales trailer at Scottish Farmers' Markets and events. Order at Farmers' Markets, email, phone and mail order. Member: Scottish Association Farmers' Markets. Email: tombuie@tombuie.com Web: www.tombuie.com. Find us at the Farmers' Market at: Aberdeen / Forfar / Edinburgh / Glasgow / Lomond Shores / Falkirk / Kilsyth / Greenock / Kirkintilloch / Aberfeldy / Stirling.

LAMB AND MUTTON

Balkissock Farm	Ballantrae	John Scott	01465 831296
Binn Farm	Glenfarg	Colin MacGregor	01577 830305
Glenearn Home Farm	Bridge of Earn	Jim Fairlie	01738 813900
Mrs Hamilton's Beef & Lamb	Kirknewton	Graham & Caroline Hamilton	01506 881510

Tender succulent organic beef and lamb. Our lamb and beef is traditionally reared and grazed on natural, organic hill, moorland and pasture and matured and butchered on the farm. All cuts are available, from joints on or off the bone to a selection of hand-made sausages and burgers. Order at Farm Shop at the farm, Farmers' Markets, email, phone and mail order. Member: Scottish Association Farmers' Markets; SOPA. Email: mrshamilton@cairnsfarm.co.uk Web: www.cairnsfarm.co.uk. Find us at the Farmers' Markets at: Edinburgh.

Neil Caskie & Sons	Greenock	Neil Caskie	01475 725531
Peelham Farm Produce	Foulden	Chris Walton	01890 781328

OSTRICH MEAT

Bellour Ostriches	Perth	Barry Lambert	01738 840236
Kezie UK Ltd	Duns	Walter Murray	01361 884006

We supply a arrange of quality Ostrich meat products: Steak Burgers in 4 & 2 packs; Roasts in various sizes; Fillet steak in 250g packs; Sausages in 300g packs; Stir Fry / Stewing steak in 350g pack; Mince in 500g packs and Liver in 350g packs. Order at Farmers' Markets, email, phone and mail order. Member: Scottish Association Farmers' Markets. Email: info@kezie.com Web: www.keziemeats.com. Find us at the Farmers' Markets at: Glasgow / Paisley / Berwick on Tweed / Edinburgh / Haddington / Peebles.

OSTRICH MEAT CONTINUED...

Moray Ostriches	Moray	Alasdair Boyne	01343 842819
Moray Ostriches	Thornhill	Kenneth Morris	01421 495390
Nellfield Farming Co	Carluke	Eileen Gibson	01555 771757

PLANTS AND HERBS

Border Belles	Innerwick	Gillian Moynihan	01368 840325
Briar Cottage Nursery	Aberfeldy	Sheena Stanbridge	01887 830362
Burngrains Nursery	Banff	John Smith	01466 780273
CC Plants	Abernethy	Catherine Fawcett	01738 850420
Caledonian Heathers and Alpines	Lossiemouth	R J Chalmers	01343 810183
Dykes Farm Nursery	Hawick	Pippa McCarter	01450 870323
Gemmas Plants	Perth	Peter Milne	01738 860653
Huntly Herbs	Huntly	Fiona Wilson	01466 720427
Ordia Nursery	Forfar	Leonie Farmer	01307 850408
Scotherbs	Longforgan	Robert Wilson	01382 360640

Scotherbs is a family business situated in the valley of the River Tay, mid-way between Perth and Dundee. Scotherbs are the major grower and suppliers of fresh culinary herbs in Scotland, supplying supermarkets, wholesale markets and of course the discerning home cook. The Company has introduced a portfolio of new products including Fresh Herb Pesto, Mustards, Salsas and Salad Dressings. Order at Farmers' Markets, email, phone and mail order. Member: British Herb Trade Association.

Email: scotherbs@compuserve.com Web: www.scotherbs.co.uk. Find us at the Farmers' Markets at: Edinburgh, plus Dundee Food and Flower Festival and the Royal Highland Show, Edinburgh.

| John Train & Sons | Tarbolton | Adam Train | 01292 541336 |

PORK AND BACON

Ballancrief Rare Breed Pigs	Ballencrief		01875 870551
Puddledub Pork & Fifeshire			
Bacon Co.	Kirkcaldy	Tom Mitchell	01592 780246
Reiver Country Foods	Eyemouth	Adam Marshall	01890 761355

POULTRY AND EGGS

Bellour Ostriches	Methven	Barrry Lambert	01778 840236
Corrie Mains Free Range Eggs	Mauchline	John Smillie	01290 550338
Country Ways	Campbeltown	Catherine Ralston	01586 820220

POULTRY AND EGGS CONTINUED...

Debbie McBean	Nairn	Debbie McBean	01309 651206
Gartmorn Farm Poultry	Alloa	Susan Jenkins	01259 750549

Gartmorn Farm produce wonderful flavoursome poultry, including free range turkeys, ducks, geese and chickens. Packs available include Turkey and Chive sausages, Diced Turkey Thigh Meat, Oven Ready Turkeys, Turkey Burgers, Chicken Drumsticks, Oven ready Chickens, Whole Duck, Oven Ready geese and many more items. Order at Farmers' Markets, email, phone or mail order. Email: susan@gartmornfarm.co.uk Web: www.gartmornfarm.co.uk, Find us at the Farmers' Markets at: Perth / Glasgow / Cupar / Clarkston / Kirkcaldy.

Gatts Fresh Farm Eggs	Banff	Jim Gatt	01261 821434
Gloagburn Free Range Eggs	Tibbermore	Ian Niven	01738 840228
Helmsdale Smokehouse	Helmsdale	Alexander Cowie	01431 821370
Highland Geese	Ardfern		01852 500609
Kintaline Plant and Poultry Centre	Oban	Jill Bowis	01631 720223

Breeders of rare utility pure bred chickens and ducks which produce an amazing array of egg colours. Plus Jacob sheep producing great meat, wool and rugs. Homegrown herbs, alpines and herbaceous plants, too! Open to the public all year. See tour website for details. Order at Farmers' Markets. Member: Scottish Association Farmers' Markets. Email: sfmc@kintaline.co.uk Web: www.kintaline.co.uk. Find us at the Farmers' Markets at: Oban/ Ardfern plus local Highland games and agricultural shows. Farm open daily to the public.

Keydon Cottage	Brechin	A Watson	01356 622953
Knowes Farm	Dunbar	Hilary Cochran	01620 860010
Oxenrig Free Range Eggs	Coldstream	Peter Calder	01890 882360
Traditional Farm Poultry	Yarrow	Shirley Black	01750 82244
Tombuie Smokehouse	Aberfeldy	David Crystal	01887 820127

PRESERVES

Braeside Apiaries	Penicuik	John Troop	01968 674947
Caledonian Curry Co	Bonar Bridge	Ian Smith	01863 766025
Mary Chalmers Preserves	Banff	Mary Chalmers	01466 751215
Graemes Ayrshire Honey	Catrine	Graeme Sharp	01290 552015
Isabellas Preserves	Ellon	Alastair Massie	01651 806257
Knowehead Products	Newburgh	Alison Batchelor	01337 841090
Rose Cottage Country Kitchen	Nairn	Katrina Ashford	01667 455671

Quality home-made jams, marmalades and chutneys along with a range of mustards, oils, vinegars and puddings. Full of fruit and flavour! Order at Farmers' Markets, email, phone and mail order. Email: k.ashford1@btinternet.com Web: www.rosecottagekitchem.co.uk. Find us at the Farmers' Markets at: Inverness / Dingwall.

The Jam Kitchen	S. Queensferry	John Sinclair	0131 319 1048

MARKET LOCATIONS

The following list, with the names of the towns currently holding a Farmers' Market describes those that are held on a regular, monthly basis. A few of the Markets are seasonal and one or two currently operate on a Sunday.

You may also find that there are a few events and fairs that hold extra markets throughout the year. Please check at your nearest Market for details about the site and operation of Markets at other locations before setting out to visit.

TOWN	DATE
Aberdeen	Last Saturday
Airdrie	1st Saturday
Angus (Forfar)	2nd Saturday
Ardrishaig	2nd Saturday
Ayr	1st Saturday
Banff	Last Saturday
Banchory	3rd Saturday
Blairgowrie	Occasional
Campbeltown	1st Saturday
Clarkston	4th Saturday
Coatbridge	2nd Saturday
Cupar	2nd Saturday
Dundee	3rd Saturday (Mar – Oct)
Dunfermline	3rd Saturday
Edinburgh	1st & 3rd Saturday
Elgin	Last Saturday
Falkirk	2nd Sunday
Forfar	2nd Saturday
Glasgow	2nd & 4th Saturday
Greenock	3rd Saturday
Haddington	Last Saturday
Hamilton	3rd Saturday
Inverness	1st Saturday
Irvine	2nd Saturday
Kelso	4th Saturday
Kilmarnock	3rd Saturday
Kilsyth	1st Saturday
Kirkcaldy	Last Saturday
Kirkwall	Occasional
Largs	4th Saturday
Lochaber	3rd Saturday
Loch Lomond Shores	3rd Sunday
Paisley	Last Saturday
Peebles	2nd Saturday
Perth	1st Saturday
Rothsay	Last Saturday
Stirling	2nd Saturday
Stornoway	Occasional
Tain	Last Saturday
Tarbert	3rd Saturday
Uist & Benbecula	Occasional

WHAT'S IN SEASON

The majority of meat and poultry is available throughout the year without specific peaks – with the exception perhaps of the demand for Christmas turkey or goose – with some fish and game being offered according to natural availability and seasons, such as wild salmon and specific game birds such as grouse, etc.

Certain fruits and vegetables are best at specific times of the year, but traditional growing and harvesting periods can now be extended through the use of poly tunnels or carefully controlled storage. The following is an indication of the prime months that you will find most of the goods listed at the Markets. If you are seeking any particular item of produce, please ask the producers at your local Market about availability and they will be happy to advise.

PRODUCE	SEASON	PRODUCE	SEASON
Apples	Sept – Dec	Lettuce	May – Oct
Asparagus	May – June	Mangetout	June – Aug
Beans (Broad)	June – July	Mushrooms	All year round
Beans (French)	July – Sept	Parsnips	Sept – Dec
Beans (Runner)	June – Oct	Pears	Sept – Oct
Beetroot	June – Nov	Peas (Shell)	June – Aug
Blackberries	July – Sept	Peas (Sugar snap)	July – Aug
Blueberries	July – Sept	Plums	Aug – Sept
Broccoli (Purple)	Feb – April	Potatoes	May – Nov
Broccoli (Green)	June – Dec	Pumpkins	Sept – Nov
Brussels Sprouts	Sept – Mar	Radishes	Apr – Nov
Cabbage	Sept – Apr	Rhubarb	Feb – May
Carrots	May – Nov	Onions	July – Oct
Cauliflower	All year round	Raspberries	June – Sept
Celeriac	Sept – Dec	Shallots	Aug – Dec
Celery	July – Dec	Spinach	May – Dec
Courgettes	June – Nov	Spring greens	Mar – Dec
Cucumbers	June – Sept	Strawberries	June – Aug
Fennel	July – Sept	Summer squash	June – Oct
Garlic	July – Sept	Swede	Sept – Dec
Gooseberries	June – Aug	Tomatoes	July – Oct
Herbs (Annuals)	July – Sept	Turnips	June – Nov
Herbs (Perennials)	All year round	Watercress	Mar – Oct
Kale	Sept – Mar	Winter squash	Oct – Dec
Leeks	Sept – Apr		

The above guide shows the peak season when you can expect to find the produce at its best, not the availability of any one item of produce. Of course, many items are suitable for freezing to enjoy out of the peak time, though please note that some produce, such as apples, should be prepared before freezing. Use all frozen fruits and vegetables as soon as practical, as storage times are not indefinite.

Certain varieties of produce will also be available at varying times, and again, if you are seeking a special favourite, please enquire with your preferred supplier who will be able to advise you further.

USEFUL CONTACTS

Scottish Association of Farmers' Markets
www.scottishfarmersmarkets.co.uk

National Association of Farmers Markets
www.farmersmarkets.net

The Soil Association
www.soilassociation.org

The Countryside Agency
www.countryside.gov.uk

Scottish Tourist Board
www.visitscotland.com

INTERNET SHOPPING SITES

www.thefoody.com

www.bigbarn.co.uk

www.realproduce.co.uk

www.farmshopping.com

www.aboutfood.com

WEIGHTS AND MEASURES CHART

WHEN COOKING, USE EITHER THE IMPERIAL OR METRIC
EQUIVALENT. DO NOT MIX THE TWO METHODS TOGETHER
IN THE SAME RECIPE. PLEASE NOTE THAT CONVERSIONS
BELOW ARE NOT AN EXACT EQUIVALENT.

Weights:

15g (½ oz)
30g (1oz)
55g (2 oz)
85g (3 oz)
100g (3½ oz)
115g (4oz)
140g (5oz)
170g (6oz)
200g (7oz)
225g (8oz)
300g (10½ oz)
340g (12oz)
400g (14oz)
450g (1lb)
500g (1lb 2oz)
550g (1¼ lb)
600g (1lb 5oz)
675g (1½ lb)
800g (1¾ lb)
900g (2lb)
1kg (2¼ lb)
1.25kg (2¾ lb)
1.5kg (3lb 3oz)
2kg (4½ lb)

1 teaspoon (tsp) = 5ml
1 tablespoon (tbsp) = 15ml

Volume:

5ml (1tsp)
10ml (2tsp)
15ml (3tsp or 1 tbsp)
22ml (1½ tbsp)
30ml (2 tbsp)
45ml (3 tbsp)
60ml (4 tbsp or ¼ cup)
75ml (2½ fl oz)
90ml (3fl oz)
100ml (3½ fl oz)
120ml (4fl oz or ½ cup)
150ml (5fl oz)
200ml (7fl oz)
250ml (8½ fl oz or 1 cup)
300ml (10fl oz)
360ml (12fl oz)
400ml (14fl oz)
450ml (15fl oz)
500ml (17fl oz exact)
600ml (1pt)
750ml (1¼ pt)
900ml (1½ pt)
1L (2pt)
1.5L (2¾ pt)
2L (3½ pt)

COOKING SPECIFICATIONS

Eggs   Unless specified, use medium eggs.

Milk   Unless specified, use whole milk.

Nuts   A few recipes may call for the use of nuts. If you
                        have, or feel you may have, an allergy to them,
                        refrain from using them in the recipe. You can
                        adapt the majority of recipes without detracting
                        from the overall result by their omission.

Oven Temperatures   Temperatures refer to gas or electric ovens. If you use
                        an aga or convection oven you should use either the
                        appropriate oven or adjust the setting according to
                        manufacturers instructions.

Oil   If using olive oil, note that this will give a flavour to
                        dishes that may vary from that using a good quality
                        vegetable oil, such as sunflower. Olive oil is best
                        reserved for use in salad dressings, pasta dressings
                        or where the flavour of the oil is the desired effect.

Herbs   Use fresh whenever possible. If using dried, reduce the
                        quantity accordingly. Salt and pepper where used
                        should be freshly ground and adjusted to taste.

Measures   All spoon measures should be level. Do not mix
                        metric and imperial quantities.

INDEX

NOTES

NOTES CONTINUED...

NOTES CONTINUED...

NOTES CONTINUED...